LIFE OF
ST. COLUMBAN

by

REV. JAMES WILSON, M.A.,
Society of St. Columban

DUBLIN
CLONMORE AND REYNOLDS LTD.
LONDON AGENTS
BURNS OATES & WASHBOURNE LTD.

9794

First Published 1953.

Nihil obstat.   MICHAEL O'DWYER, D.D.,
                                       Censor Theol. Deput.

Imprimi potest   ✠   JOANNES,
                                       Episcopus Midensis.
Die 6 Februarii, anno 1952.

MADE AND PRINTED IN THE
REPUBLIC OF IRELAND FOR
CLONMORE & REYNOLDS BY
SEALY BRYERS & WALKER
DUBLIN

CONTENTS

CHAPTER		PAGE
	PREFACE	7
I.	Birth and Boyhood	9
II.	Cleenish and Bangor	13
III.	Peregrinari pro Christo	17
IV.	Foundation of Annegray, Luxeuil and Fontaine	20
V.	Life in Luxeuil	25
VI.	The Rule of St. Columban	32
VII.	'Audax in Causa Veritatis'	38
VIII.	'Fortis in Tribulationibus'	44
IX.	'Wherever the way of Salvation might lead'	54
X.	In Switzerland	59
XI.	In the Court of the Lombards	65
XII.	Bobbio	73
XIII.	The Foundations Set Firm	78
	ST. COLUMBAN'S LETTER	89
	APPENDIX	96
	FOOTNOTES	102

POEM TO FEDOLIUS.

Now, dear brother Fedolius, leave aside the more florid songs of the learned, and read these trifles of ours. May Christ, the Judge of the world, the only-begotten of the Almighty, send you the gentle joys of life.

PREFACE.

Our knowledge of St. Columban comes principally from his own writings and the Life written by Jonas. His own writings, as at present accepted as genuine, are: The Rule, the Penitential, four Homilies, six Letters and six Poems. From these we can learn what kind of man he was and something about the life in his monasteries.

For the details of his life we rely chiefly on Jonas. There are many references to him in other ancient lives of saints; but they give us very little additional information, as they are, for the most part, based on Jonas.

Jonas was born in Susa, a town in northern Italy, about 120 miles west of Bobbio. He entered the monastery of Bobbio in 618, three years after St. Columban's death. The vast majority of the men with whom he lived in Bobbio had known St. Columban; and some of them, like St. Attala, had been with him in the peaceful days of Luxeuil, and had shared his long journey through France, Switzerland and into Italy. For the first ten or twelve years of Jonas' life as a monk, his duties kept him in his monastery; but later we find him on many a journey from Bobbio as far as the North Sea. We know that he often met St. Gall in Switzerland, and spoke to St. Eustasius in Luxeuil; he was a frequent visitor in the convent of St. Fara, near Paris; he heard St. Chagnoald, bishop of Laon, telling what he knew about St. Columban; and for three years he worked as a missionary on the coast of the North Sea, under St. Amand, the Apostle of Belgium. As a young monk he had been minister to the Abbots Attala and Bertulf, and as such had charge of the documents in Bobbio. It is clear that from his travels and his office in the monastery he was in a position to acquire first-hand information about St. Columban.

It was only with great reluctance that he consented to write the Life; only the constant urging of his fellow-monks and the express wish of the Abbot overcame his hesitancy. They were all anxious that the work should be done while there were still alive many who had known St. Columban.

In appraising the work of Jonas, it is important to keep in mind that many who are mentioned in his narrative were still alive when he wrote; for example, St. Eloi, St. Ouen, St. Faron, St. Donatus, St. Fara, St. Salaberga, St. Romaric. What he tells us about St. Romaric is not complimentary to that saint, who at the time of writing was abbot of Remiremont, near Luxeuil. One of the miracles of St. Columban that Jonas tells was worked in favour of the father of Bobolenus, the abbot of Bobbio, to whom Jonas dedicated his work. For some incidents Jonas gives us his authority. For every phase of St. Columban's life after he had landed in France, Jonas had some witnesses; for the later years in Luxeuil and from that to the end, he had literally hundreds. It was principally for the communities of these men that Jonas wrote.

In the following pages, all quotations not otherwise attributed are from Jonas. No use has been made of later legends, however beautiful and attractive, lest uncertainty cloud the picture.

Chapter I.

BIRTH AND BOYHOOD.

ST. COLUMBAN was born in the province of Leinster, Ireland, about the year 530. We cannot be more definite about the place of his birth, but it was probably in the Carlow-Kildare region. The date is more important. Some of the very old people of his young days had been born in paganism, and there were many whose parents had been pagans; the stories about St. Patrick and the extraordinary outpourings of grace in the first days of the faith in Ireland were commonplace around the firesides. Not far from his home was the great school of Kildare, where St. Brigid had died a few years before he was born.

Though the rapid spread of the faith in Ireland is outstanding in mission history, and though there had been many saints in the seventy years that had gone by since St. Patrick died, yet, as Jonas truly says, ' the seeds of the faith had not yet all fructified.' It was during the boyhood days of St. Columban that the full flowering of the faith was seen. Columkille, Enda, Fintan, Finian, Kevin, Ita, Jarlath and many of the numerous Colmans were leading hundreds and thousands to the love of God in the great schools that they were then founding in all parts of the country. Into that flood-tide of grace Columban was born.

About his family we know very little. There is a hint that his father's name was also Columban; we know nothing more about him. There is no mention of any brothers or sisters. When he left home there must have been someone to support his mother, otherwise, according to the Canon Law of the time, he would not be admitted into any ecclesiastical institute. The younger St. Columban, of whose holy death we shall read, was a cousin of his. It is only of his mother that Jonas gives us any information.

A short time before he was born she had a dream, in which she saw a great light shining from her breast. She asked some of the neighbours what they thought it meant. They told her that, in their opinion, it meant that the child to be born was destined to bring the light of faith to many. She kept the dream in mind, and the interpretation that had been given; and when her son was born, she determined to do what she could to fit him for the work that the dream had foreshadowed. She did not follow the usual custom of handing over his care to others, but kept him at home with herself.

When the time came for him to go to school, his parents sent him to a teacher near home. For them, as for all Irish parents of the time, education meant simply the training of the child in the knowledge and the love of God; all study was directed towards that end. This does not mean that the studies were confined to the Catechism and the Bible: all creation was the work of God, and whatever was good and beautiful was but a reflex of His goodness and His beauty. He had the usual foundation of reading and writing his native language; the history of the Church and of the world, and, probably, the beginnings of astronomy; then came Latin, with its declensions and conjugations and syntax, and all the other headaches of a Latin class: Jonas tells us that Columban did not easily forget the hard hours of work he had to put into his studies. While all through his course the study of the Scriptures was paramount, especially the Gospels and the Psalms, it is abundantly clear that Columban had received a thorough grounding in the Latin classics, Virgil, Horace, Cicero and the rest.

He was about seventeen or eighteen years of age

when he decided to dedicate his life to God. He had taken to himself, without reserve, the words of Our Lord that he had read in the Gospels: "Thou shalt love the Lord thy God with thy whole heart"; "If you love Me, keep My commandments"; "Amen, I say to you, there is no man who hath left house or brethren or sisters or father or mother or children or lands, for My sake and for the Gospel, who shall not receive a hundred times as much, now in this time; houses and brethren and sisters and mothers and children and lands, with persecutions: and in the world to come life everlasting"; "I am come to cast fire on the earth. And what will I, but that it be kindled." He would leave nothing undone to save his own soul, and would follow Our Lord along whatever path He might lead, even though it cost him the sacrifice of father and mother and home.

His difficulty now was, how and where he would serve God. He probably realised that the people at home could not give an unbiased opinion on these points. His father and mother were good Catholics, but their love for him would naturally induce them to suggest any alternative that would keep him near them. In his trouble, he went to consult an old woman who had lived as a hermit for many years and who had acquired a reputation for good judgment. He told her all about himself, what he wished to do, and the temptations that he feared. Her answer was definite: if he really meant to follow Our Lord, he would have to cut himself off from the dangers that were around him; he would have to leave home. He accepted her advice and determined to follow it.

He told some of his companions, and then faced the ordeal at home. He knew how much he owed to his mother; he was old enough to realise that she had been far more careful of his upbringing and his education than was usual; he knew that her heart was set on him, and he certainly returned her love. But the words of Our Lord were clear: "He that loveth father or mother more than Me is not worthy of Me." When he told her what he intended to do, she implored him not to leave her. He reminded her of Our Lord's words; but all to no avail. Even when the day for leaving had come she continued to beg of him to stay near home; and as he was leaving the house she stood at the door to stop him. Jonas tells us that he stepped over her, as she lay prostrate at the door. Whether that expression is to be taken literally or figuratively, matters little: it was a heart-breaking wrench for both.

Chapter II.

CLEENISH AND BANGOR.

HE went first to a small school in the island of Cleenish, in Lough Erne, which was conducted by a saintly man named Sinell. It was not a monastery in the ordinary sense, but would correspond rather to a philosophy seminary.[1] Here he continued his studies in the Scriptures, Church History and Latin. ' Such progress did he make in his sacred studies that, while yet a young man, he wrote a finished work on the Psalms, and also some other works, hymns and books of instructions.' There is still extant a Commentary on the Psalms, which is said to be St. Columban's; but its authenticity is doubtful. Jonas gives us an interesting, and familiar, side-light on class-work in Cleenish: ' As often happens when masters wish to test the ability of their students, or to check their negligence, or to clarify the matter in hand, Sinell would sometimes ask Columban for an explanation of the more difficult passages. And he, not wishing to disobey, would put questions himself, though timidly and without any show of ostentation.' Apparently calls in class have not changed much in fourteen hundred years.

We do not know how long he remained in Cleenish; probably about five years, possibly more. He had now more definite ideas about his future, and applied for admission to the monastery of Bangor, then recently founded by St. Comgall. It was situated on the southern shore of what is now Belfast Lough. His choice of Bangor was probably influenced by the fact that Sinell and St. Comgall were friends. Jonas tells us that 'Abbot Comgall, renowned for his great sanctity, was the outstanding father of monks in Ireland, and was known for his insistence on study and strict discipline.' Comgall had been trained in a hard school, that of St. Fintan of Clonenagh, where the rule proved too much even for some of the giants of those days. But Bangor, under St. Comgall, soon became known as 'Bangor of the kindly rule'; discipline was maintained, but the fatherly rule of Comgall made the burden light. The old hymn of the seventh century begins:

> Benchuir bona regula,
> Recta atque divina;
> Stricta, sancta, sedula,
> Summa, justa ac mira.[2]

It must have admirably suited a man of Columban's temperament. Years later we find Luxeuil with the same reputation throughout France: a place where men of good-will, dissatisfied with the laxity of other monasteries, could serve God in the security of discipline, under a kindly master.

Bangor was a monastery in the ordinary sense of the word, where, after a period of probation, the usual vows were taken. The Abbot's word was law; and no one could leave the monastery or take up any work without his permission. It must be remembered that the monastery of Bangor had only one end in view: the spiritual good of the individual; it did not aim specifically at training contemplatives or missionaries or teachers, though doubtless the training did tend to develop the individual natural gifts of the members. As we have said, the monk could not leave the monastery without the Abbot's permission, and while in the Abbey he lived the life of a monk; yet there was nothing to prevent the subject from asking, nor the Abbot from granting, permission to leave the monastery and take up any kind of work to which it seemed that God was calling him. Some, with the sanction of the Abbot, were called to the priesthood; and it was here that Columban was ordained priest.

Jonas tells us practically nothing of St. Columban's life in Bangor. But tradition says that he was head of the school; and, also, *anam-chara* (soul-friend) or spiritual director.

'After he had passed many years in Bangor, the desire to go into exile began to grow in him, for he remembered the words of God to Abraham: Go forth out of thy country and from thy kindred, and out of thy father's house, and come into the land which I shall show thee.'[3] The stories of the early martyrs of the Church were well known in the monasteries and schools of Ireland, but little hope could be entertained that God would call on His servants for the supreme sacrifice, at least in their native land. Hence they had to be content with what they called ' white martyrdom ': if they could not imitate the early martyrs in the shedding of their blood, they would show their love by the sacrifice of all that was dear to them. Even in the earlier days of the faith in Ireland the desire to ' peregrinari pro Christo ' was not unknown. It was not intended merely as an act of mortification; it included a readiness and a desire to spread the knowledge and the love of God in the hearts of all men, to bring life and to bring it more abundantly. Columban ' therefore made known to the Abbot Comgall the wishes and the ardent longing that had been enkindled in him by that fire of which Our Lord speaks: I have come to cast fire on the earth, and what will I, but that it be kindled? Comgall, however, did not readily give his consent. He realized what a great loss Columban would be to Bangor. But as he turned over the matter in his mind, he saw that he should not place his own interests above those of his neighbour; and that Divine Providence had trained this young soldier for the wars, to bring back in triumph the spoils of his vanquished enemies. He, therefore, called Columban and made known to him his decision: he would give him permission and his blessing; he would provide him with whatever was necessary, and would give him worthy companions of his exile.' The names of some of the twelve who were selected to accompany St. Columban have come down to us: St. Columban the younger, St. Gall, St. Deicola, Comin, Eunog, Eogain and Lua. St. Columban was about forty years of age when he left Bangor.

Chapter III.

PEREGRINARI PRO CHRISTO.

THEY had no particular destination in mind when they left Bangor.[4] They probably first landed in Cornwall, where they rested for a short while, still ' undecided what they should do. At length it seemed best to go into Gaul, and, if conditions were favourable, to stay there awhile and preach; but if they found the people unreceptive, to move on to some of the neighbouring peoples. They therefore left Britain and went into Gaul.'

Without going into any great detail on the complicated political condition of Gaul at the time, it is necessary to give some idea of the people among whom Columban and his friends were to work. The Franks, who ruled the country, had been Catholics for about seventy years, their ruler, Clovis, having been baptized in 496. But he, and more especially his successors, were too prone to look upon themselves as rulers of the Church as well as of the State; and far too frequently used their great influence to have their own creatures, however unworthy, appointed as bishops. The result was that in very many cases men were appointed who cared little for the welfare of the Church, and who were a scandal to the people. It must be remembered, however, that there were some zealous and saintly bishops in Gaul, through whose influence many of the people were eager to listen to the word of God. To complicate matters, the Burgundians in the east, who were subject to the Franks, had been baptized in the Arian heresy. To complete the chaotic picture, dying paganism began to show signs of reviving; there are many instances

in Gaul in the sixth century, and St. Columban was
to meet it on the Swiss-Austrian border and even in
northern Italy. St. Bertulf, who was elected third
Abbot of Bobbio in 625, was born of pagan parents.
Against paganism, heresy and scandal in high places,
only men whose lives spoke the message of the Gospel
in all its fullness, and whose courage was strong
against the malice of the mighty, could hope to win
souls for God.

As we have said, they had no fixed programme
when they landed in Gaul; they would stay and preach
wherever conditions were favourable. They remained
for a short time in Brittany, where their visit is still
remembered. Then they went east through France.
' Wherever he went, Columban took care to preach
the Gospel. The eloquence of his preaching and the
example of his virtues induced men to listen to him.'
As they went on, they made a deep impression on all
who met them, especially by their humility, their
patience and the strong bond of friendship that united
them. ' So abundant were the graces that Heaven had
bestowed on Columban, that in whatever home he
stayed he drew all to the service of God.' So Jonas
hands on to us what he had heard from those who had
known St. Columban. It was not merely his eloquence,
however impressive, and his sanctity, however inspiring, but also his deep personal interest in all who came
under his influence, that led men to follow him.

As they went eastwards through France, their fame
went before them, and they were well received by
Sigibert, the king of Austrasia, the most easterly kingdom of the Franks. He urged them to settle down in
his territories, and promised to provide them with
whatever they might need. Columban hesitated: he
did not wish to enrich himself at the expense of others,
and said that he merely wished to settle down in some
secluded place, where he and his friends could serve

God in peace. The king understood his difficulty, but replied: ' If you wish to take up the Cross of Christ and follow Him, seek a more secluded place, but do not leave our territories; thus you will at once increase your own reward and will help us towards salvation.' Columban yielded to the king's request, and began to look for a site more suitable to his needs. ' In a wild desolate region in the Vosges mountains was a dilapidated fort called Annegray. When Columban saw the place he settled down there, though it was dreary and desolate and overrun with brushwood.'

CHAPTER IV.

FOUNDATION OF ANNEGRAY, LUXEUIL
AND FONTAINE.

WHEN the Romans had conquered that section of
Gaul, they built a number of forts at strategic
points. Annegray was one of these; but subsequent incursions of the barbarians had again reduced
the place to a wilderness, where the wild beasts of the
forest roamed at will. Even to-day the visitor can
easily understand how secure from intrusion Columban
must have felt in the place he had chosen. The site
of the old monastery is now cultivated, and there are
villages scattered along the banks of the river Breuchin
that flows in the valley; but the forest hills that rise
rugged and dense and wild make it easy for the
imagination to picture again that ' no man's land ' that
then separated the kingdoms of Austrasia and Burgundy.

They settled down in that ' desert,' as Jonas calls
it, and began to build some kind of shelter, living on
whatever they could gather in the woods. As might
be expected, food obtained in this way was not very
sustaining, especially for the sick. ' While they were
there, one of the group fell ill of a fever. As the only
food they had was the bark of some trees and a few
herbs, they began to fast and pray that they might be
able to get some nourishing food for the sick man.
They had fasted for three days and were nearly
exhausted, when they saw a man coming towards
them, leading horses laden with bread. He came and
stood at the door and told them that it had suddenly

occurred to him to bring help to those who were in need because of their love of God. When he had given the bread to Columban, he asked him to pray for his wife, who had now been a year sick, and there was little hope for her recovery. The man of God could not refuse his humble and earnest prayer; he called the others and together they prayed for the sick woman. No sooner had they finished their prayer than the sick woman was restored to health; for when the husband, having received the blessing of Columban, had returned home, he found his wife sitting up, well; and, on making enquiries, he discovered that the fever had left her at the moment that Columban and his friends prayed for her.'

Jonas tells us of a somewhat similar incident, about this same time, that made Annegray and its monks better known. 'One time, when they had been for nine days without food, except the bark of trees and herbs, the Abbot of the monastery of Salix,[5] whose name was Carantocus, was told by God in a dream to send help to His servant, Columban, who was living in the desert. When he awoke, he told his cellarer, Marculf, what had happened. "Better do as you were told," said Marculf. Carantocus thereupon ordered Marculf to get together whatever he could and bring it to Columban. Marculf loaded his carts and set out. When he came to the beginning of the forest, he could not see any path or trail; but, realising that if the command had come from God, He would show a way, he allowed the horses to go forward; and they made their way straight to the door of Columban at Annegray. Marculf followed the horses and delivered the supplies to Columban, who gave thanks to God, Who had not failed to furnish a table for His servants in the desert. Marculf received his blessing and returned home by the way he had come, telling everyone what had happened. After that, crowds of people, and especially the sick, began to throng to Annegray, seeking a cure for their ailments. Columban prayed for them, and, by the power of God, cured them.'

Soon the road to Annegray became well known, and the days of compulsory fasting were over. The vast majority of their visitors would have come a long journey—the immediate vicinity was practically uninhabitable—and it was necessary to provide additional accommodation. Many had to remain overnight, and thus provided Columban with an opportunity to speak to them individually. His sincere interest in all their troubles quickly won their hearts, and thus began what must be regarded as one of his outstanding achievements of grace, the power to inspire the hearts of those who came under his influence with the sheer love of God. We nowhere read that St. Columban had any special efficacy in preaching to crowds, and the life led at Annegray could not have been an attraction to the unconverted; but once Providence had given him the opportunity to speak to the individual, either in the homes at which he stayed or in the quiet of his own cloisters, his words had an extraordinary appeal and drew many, very many, after him on the road to heroic sanctity.

He has told us that he had two desires, apparently contradictory: to lead a life of solitude, and to bring the love of God to others. The great influx of visitors to Annegray gave him an opportunity to satisfy one of his desires; but those same crowds directly interfered with the other. He remembered that Our Blessed Lord had often retired from ' active ' work to pray in secret, and that He had recommended the same practice to His Apostles. ' One day when he had penetrated farther than usual into the woods, he came upon a huge rock, the front of which had broken off, thus forming a cave. When he examined it more closely, he found that it was a bear's den, and the

bear was inside. The gentle saint ordered the ferocious
beast to depart and never come there again. The bear
went off and made its den about seven miles from
Annegray, and never molested them.'

' It became the custom with Columban to retire to
this cave on Sundays and before the feasts of saints, to
give himself to uninterrupted prayer. In this way he
was able to lay aside for a while the care of others,
and retire for quiet meditation. He had a young boy,
named Domualis, to help him and to bring messages
to and from the monastery. On one occasion, when
Columban had been for several days in the cave,
Domualis began to grumble, under his breath, that
the well was too far away, and that he was worn out
dragging the water all the way up the hill. Columban
said to him: " Son, try the rock; remember that the
Lord drew water from the rock for the children of
Israel." As the boy approached the rock, Columban
fell on his knees and prayed to God to come to their
aid. Kind Providence heard his prayer: water began
to come from the rock, and soon there was a constant flow, that continues to the present day.' So
wrote Jonas more than thirteen hundred years ago;
and the water still flows. The cave is now a place of
pilgrimage, and a small chapel has been built close
by. The pilgrim will have no difficulty in believing
that bears once roamed those mountains, and the boy's
complaints will have his full sympathy.

The crowds continued to come to Annegray, and
many applied to be received into the community.
Additional buildings were erected, but soon they, too,
were overcrowded. Finally Columban decided that
another foundation was necessary. He set off along
the banks of the Breuchin to look for a suitable site,
and about seven miles from Annegray he came upon
the ruins of what had once been the important Roman
town of Luxovium, famous in Caesar's time for its

natural hot baths. The invasions of the barbarians had ended its glory, and, when Columban first saw it, it was a complete ruin, where weeds and brushwood covered the debris of pagan worship. There he made his second foundation, and there he took up residence, leaving a prior in charge of Annegray. In course of time Luxeuil, too, was overcrowded, and St. Columban built his third monastery at a place which he named Fontaine, about four miles west of Luxeuil; there, too, he placed a prior in charge.

All three, Annegray, Luxeuil and Fontaine, remained down to the French Revolution. Of Annegray nothing is left, but the site is marked by a cross. At Fontaine there are some remains of the later monastery buildings and the prior's house, which is still in use as a dwellinghouse. In Luxeuil, the old Abbey Church, which has now the rank of a Basilica, serves as the parish church; a large part of the monastery buildings now houses a minor seminary for the Archdiocese of Besançon, where the memory and the spirit of St. Columban still remain.

Chapter V.

LIFE IN LUXEUIL.

WITHIN a short time of its foundation, Luxeuil began to be crowded with applicants for admission as monks, and its school became favourably known far and wide. Many of the boys whose parents had entrusted them to St. Columban remained under his charge as monks, and proved by their lives that his teaching was not in vain. We will mention two. One of the local rulers, named Waldelenus, had no children, and he and his wife came to Columban, to ask his prayers that God might bless their union. Columban promised his prayers, but stipulated that they should agree to dedicate their first child to God: if they did so, God would send them other children. They promised, and in due course a son was born to them. He was brought to Columban and was given the name Donatus. When he was about ten years old, he was sent to the school of Luxeuil, where he ultimately lived as a monk, until his appointment as bishop of Besançon, a position he held when Jonas was writing his life of St. Columban. His feast is celebrated in Besançon on August 7th.

One of the companions of St. Donatus in Luxeuil was a boy named Agilus, whose father, Cagnoald, was an influential courtier of the king, and had helped St. Columban at the foundation of Luxeuil. On a visit to the home of Cagnoald, St. Columban had seen the boy, then about seven years old, and predicted that he would one day be a good soldier of Christ. A few years later he was sent to the school of Luxeuil, later entered as a monk, preached as a missionary in Bavaria, and was the first abbot of the monastery of Rebais. His feast is on August 30.

Unfortunately, Jonas does not give us any detail about life in the school of Luxeuil. He does, however, give us some interesting stories about life in the monastery. St. Gall told him one against himself. One day, when he and St. Columban were in the ' desert,' probably in the hinterland to the east of Annegray, St. Columban told him to go and fish in the river Breuchin. Gall went off, but, like many another fisherman, knew a better hole, and went to the river L'Ognon. ' He cast his net and saw a great shoal of fish coming, but he could not catch any; as soon as they came to the net, they turned back, as if they had come up against a wall. All day long he tried, but caught nothing. He went back and told Columban of his failure. "Why did you not go where you were told?" said Columban. "Go back now to the Breuchin." He went back quickly, set his net, and caught such a multitude of fish that the net could scarcely hold them all. Gall himself told me of this incident.'

' Once when Columban had retired to the cave from which he had driven the bear, and had spent many days in prayer and fasting, it was made known to him by Heaven that many of the monks in Luxeuil were sick, and that there were only enough left to take care of the invalids. He returned at once, and ordered all to arise and thrash the harvest. Those who were strong in obedience arose at once and set about thrashing the harvest with confidence. When Columban saw their faith and obedience: " Stop," he said, " you must be worn out from sickness and work; you need refreshment." Those who had obeyed noticed with surprise that no trace of their sickness remained; and Columban ordered a meal to be prepared that they might refresh themselves. He then reproved the disobedient for their want of confidence, and warned them that their sickness would be of long duration. For a whole year their sickness continued, and thus they expiated their disobedience by penance.'

Increasing numbers made it necessary for them each year to clear additional sections of the forest for new planting. ' One harvest time Columban happened to be in Fontaine, where a new field had yielded an excellent crop. The time had come to gather the harvest, but there was such continuous wind and rain that there was danger that the grain might be shed and the harvest lost. Columban was at a loss what to do; but his strong faith came to the rescue. He ordered everything to be made ready and summoned the monks to the reaping. They were all surprised, but none mentioned his surprise to Columban. They set out with their scythes, in a downpour of rain, meantime watching to see what Columban was doing. At the four corners of the field he had stationed four monks of tried virtue: three Irishmen, Comin, Eunog and Eogain, and one Briton, named Gurgan. Then he took his place among the reapers and began to reap with them. Though the rain continued to fall all around them, not a drop fell where they worked; but a hot sun shone out and a warm breeze blew, until the harvest was cut.'

Jonas was over-sensitive to criticism, and, before telling the next incident, he feels that an apologia is necessary. ' If I here make mention of some things that seem petty, I leave myself open to the sneers of the disparager. But the goodness of God is seen in small things as well as in great; He listens to our prayers in things of little importance as He does in serious matters.' That apologia is sometimes necessary even now. There are some who think that Jonas is too ready to accept the miraculous. They forget that here is question of one of the greatest of the saints, whose life was marked, not by eloquent appeal to the kings and rulers of the earth, nor by a genius for organizing a great society, but by his power to win the heart of the individual who came to him and to carry him with him to the heights of sanctity. It should not be surprising if Columban often used his great influence with our Father in Heaven, to help those who called him father on earth, even in the little things of life. Here, then, is the story that Jonas tells.

'One day Columban and some of the monks were reaping at a farm called Banaritia[6]—it was a good day for reaping, with a gentle breeze from the south—when one of them, named Theudegile, happened to cut his figner with the scythe, so badly that only a small piece of skin kept it together. Columban noticed him standing, and told him to keep on working. Then Theudegile told him what had happened. He rushed to him at once, touched the finger with a little saliva, and it was immediately cured. Theudegile himself told me of this incident, and showed me the finger.'

Another day, one of the neighbours, a man named Winioc, was watching the monks preparing timber in the forest. He was noticing how easily they were able to split the trunk of an oak with wedges, when a splinter flew and cut him very badly on the forehead. St. Columban saw that it was a dangerous wound; he fell upon his knees, then touched the wound and healed it. That man's son, Bobolenus, was Abbot of Bobbio when Jonas was a monk there, and was one of those to whom he dedicated his life of St. Columban.

We are told in the Scriptures that before the Fall man had control over the lower animals. They would come at his call and would obey his orders. It would seem that the nearer one now approaches in sanctity to the state of original justice, the greater participation in the gifts of that state does God give to

His servant. We have many examples in the lives of the saints. Jonas tells us that he had often heard Chagnoald, the bishop of Laon, tell what he had seen when he was alone in the woods with Columban. Chagnoald had known St. Columban from boyhood, from the day that the saint had stayed at his father's house in La Brie, near Paris, on his journey from Nantes. Later he became a monk in Luxeuil, where he was St. Columban's minister or secretary, until his appointment as bishop. He told Jonas that ' he had often seen Columban call the birds and the wild beasts, when he would be in the "desert" for prayer and meditation. They would come at his call, and when he would rub them down gently with his hand they would frisk and gambol about him, like little puppies about their master. There was a little squirrel, too, who would come down when summoned from the top branches of the trees, and alight on his hand or his shoulder as he was entering or leaving the cave.'

Jonas gives us a particular instance of this power, not without its touch of humour. ' One day when Columban had returned from work at meal time to the monastery at Luxeuil, he left the gloves that he wore at work—the Gauls call them " wanti "—outside the door of the monastery. When all was quiet, a raven flew down and carried off one of the gloves. At the end of the meal Columban came out and looked everywhere for his glove. The monks were wondering who could have taken it; but Columban said that the only one who would have dared to take anything without permission was the bird that refused to return to Noah in the Ark: " And no more food for the young birds, until the glove is returned." While they stood there, the raven flew back with the glove in its beak, making no attempt to fly away, until Columban told it to be off.'

It should not surprise us that the Lord would grant

to those who try to imitate Him in their lives the power to imitate Him in His miracles. We have examples in the life of Columban of multiplication of food. Here is one. 'One day when Columban was at the monastery of Fontaine[7], he saw sixty of the monks hoeing the ground and preparing it for the seed. He saw that the work was hard, and said: "Stop, and take what the Lord has sent." When the bursar heard what was said, he was worried:

"But we have only two loaves and a little beer."
"Bring them to me," said Columban.
He then looked up to Heaven and prayed:

"O Christ Jesus, the one hope of the world, Who appeased the hunger of the five thousand in the desert, multiply this food and drink."

His strong faith was rewarded, and all had as much food and drink as they wished. From this and other similar instances it is clear that St. Columban was not averse to relaxing the rule when occasion demanded.

The years in Luxeuil were happy ones for St. Columban. He had seen his community increase in numbers beyond his wildest dreams; and, far more important, he saw that his work was blessed by God. Not only were there many of heroic sanctity, but the whole spirit was good. He loved them all, and he knew that they loved him. He found it very hard to see any of them leave him, even for Heaven, as the following story will show. Here is how Jonas tells it:

'In the monastery of Luxeuil, one of the monks, whose name also was Columban, was critically sick of a fever, and was praying for a happy death. When he was on the point of dying, confident of the eternal reward for which he had so long worked, he saw some one coming to him and saying: "I cannot yet take you forth from the body, for I am prevented by the prayers and the tears of your Father, Columban."

When the sick man heard that, he called the infirmarian, Theudegile, whom we have mentioned already, and said to him: "Go quickly and tell our Father Columban to come to me." The infirmarian went at once and found Columban in the church, praying and weeping. He told him that the sick man wished to see him. Columban went without delay, and asked the dying man what was it that he wished. He answered: "Why are you keeping me in this miserable world by your prayers? They are waiting to bring me to Heaven, but are prevented by your prayers and your tears. Do not continue to oppose them, for Heaven is open to receive me." Columban was struck with fear and summoned all the monks to the sick room. Their sorrow at losing their saintly companion was tempered with great joy. The Holy Viaticum was administered; the last Pax given; the chant for the dead was sung. He had the same name as Columban; he was related to him by blood, and was one of those who had come with him from Ireland.' According to an old tradition, they laid him to rest under the High Altar of the Abbey Church in Luxeuil, where the people still ask his prayers in the Litany of their own saints.

Chapter VI.

THE RULE OF ST. COLUMBAN.

WITH Annegray, Luxeuil and Fontaine now firmly established, St. Columban drew up his Rule for the government of his Abbeys. Unfortunately, it has not come down to us in its entirety; but from the writings of St. Columban himself, the Life by Jonas and other traditions, we are able to piece together the main features of life in his monasteries.

Government. The Abbot was the supreme authority, and could change the rules and the horarium at will. While St. Columban lived, he was looked upon as the superior of all the monasteries; but subsequent superiors were elected by the community, and held office for life. In the foundation charter of the monastery of Solignac the Abbot of Luxeuil is given the right of visitation; it would seem that he was granted a similar right in other monasteries also. Smaller monasteries, like Annegray and Fontaine, were ruled by priors, under the abbot of the mother-abbey. Under the abbot were a number of minor superiors, with limited authority.

Personnel. In the monastery were schoolboys, novices and professed monks. Boys were admitted at a very early age; St. Agilus, for example, was sent to the school of Luxeuil when he was ten years of age. The boys, of course, had their own regime in the monastery. As one would expect, many of them remained on and entered the monastery as novices. The novices were under their own director, and were not allowed to mix with the professed monks. After

the period of probation, if the Abbot judged favourably, they were admitted to profession, and took the
customary vows. As the monastery had no other end
in view but the spiritual development of the individual,
practically the only obstacle to profession would be
stubborn want of goodwill. After profession some were
called to the priesthood, depending on the judgment of
the abbot. The professed monk could not leave the
monastery without the permission of the abbot; but
the abbot could assign him to work outside the
monastery, for example, preaching to the pagans or
directing a newly-founded monastery. Interchange of
monks between monasteries, at least between Luxeuil
and Bobbio, was not uncommon, always with the consent of both abbots. A monk could be expelled, but
only as a last resort; those whose talk was creating
dissension were regarded as least desirable.

Daily Life. Their daily horarium was much like
that of the modern Cistercians. They rose for Matins
in the very early hours of the morning, and said the
other Hours in choir during the day. The time not
devoted to common prayer was occupied in private
prayer and the works that we always associate with
monasteries. Their morning meal was scanty; their
principal meal, taken in the evening, was substantial,
but plain: vegetables, bread, frequently fish, and, for
drink, a kind of beer. St. Columban gives us his ideas
about food and drink: ' It should be such as will
sustain the body, not injure it. In this matter we must
use discretion; for if abstinence is carried too far, it
becomes a vice, not a virtue.[8] Just as each day we
must read and work and pray, so each day we must
honour God by controlling our appetites.' We have
many instances when an extra meal was provided
because of special circumstances. Guests were entertained in the guest-house; it was the duty of the bursar
to see to their comfort; in his absence, the other monks

C

were to provide what was necessary. The number of
hours assigned to sleep is not stated; but St. Columban
realized that there were not too many. Speaking of the
life of a monk he says: ' The monk goes to bed tired,
he is already half asleep on his feet; and he is routed
out again before he has slept enough.' This is sometimes quoted to prove that the rule in Luxeuil was too
hard: the younger members of most religious institutes
to-day would readily recognise their own experience
in St. Columban's words.

Spiritual Training. The training in Luxeuil and in
the other monasteries of St. Columban had no distinc-
tive end in view. Those who came were not specially
trained to be contemplatives or teachers or missionaries
or preachers. Many, indeed, did distinguish themselves in these fields; but the desire of St. Columban
was to inspire them with such a strong love of Our
Lord that they would readily give themselves to any
work or suffering that He might call them to. The very
first words of his rule, introducing a chapter on
obedience, are: ' Primo omnium docemur Deum
diligere ex toto corde et ex tota mente. . . .' ' We are
taught first of all to love God with our whole heart,
and our whole mind. . . .'; as if to emphasise that
virtue without that foundation, solid and firm, is on
shaky ground.

The model that he set before them was, of course,
Our Lord in the Gospels. He himself had accepted
without reserve all that Our Lord had said. He had
kept His commandments, and had followed His
counsels to the full. He had heard clearly Our Lord's
prophecy that His followers would be persecuted in
this life; he heard equally clearly His promise of help
in this life, and a kingdom of happiness in the next.
When troubles came and his whole work was in
jeopardy, he felt it, and felt it keenly; but his confidence in God was not shaken. He wrote to his

monks:[9] ' What has happened to us is nothing new. This is the Gospel that we preach every day: that the true disciples of Christ crucified follow Him with the cross. Blessed is he who shares in His sufferings and in His ignominy.' When the boatmen on the Rhine looked in vain for help from their friends, St. Columban said to them: ' Now let me go to my Friend.' He went to his Friend in the church and got what was needed. As a modern writer has said: ' He was the kind of man that made Our Lord keep His word.' In little things as well as in great, he appealed to Our Lord with equal confidence. For their consolation in suffering, he reminded his followers of the words of Our Lord: ' Where I am, there also shall My minister be,' both in this life and the next. A line in one of his poems sums up his teaching in a few words:

Optimus est animus Christi vestitus amore.[10]

Obedience. If obedience is to be of any value, it must be ' ex integro et non ex parte '[11]; it must be universal, not partial; if a man decides for himself in what he will obey, he is never obedient, for he is always following his own will. What limits can be placed to obedience? St. Columban replies: ' Usque ad mortem certe praecepta est, quia Christus usque ad mortem obedivit Patri pro nobis ': we must be obedient unto death, because Christ was obedient unto death for us. If a valid command is given, it must be obeyed even at the risk of death. He does not neglect to give a sound natural motive for obedience: the position of one called on to obey is much to be preferred to that of one called on to command; the subject can carry out his orders with peace of mind, the superior has all the worry.[12] Without true humility obedience is very difficult, if not impossible; only the humble can realise that the yoke of Christ is sweet and His burden light.

C2

Mortification. In this section St. Columban confines his remarks to mortification of the will, or obedience. It would seem that St. Columban regarded the keeping of the rule and the fulfilment of duties as affording ample opportunity for mortification. More than once in his words to his monks he makes it clear that he realized that the life they were leading was not an easy one. We seldom come across instances of voluntary external mortification. We have no instance of those extraordinary mortifications that we read of so often in the lives of the early Irish saints.

Silence. His words on silence show us that St. Columban regarded it, not so much as a mortification, but rather as a training in control of the tongue, for the safety of the community. Over and over again he warns his monks to be diligent in preserving unity, and not to jeopardize it by unbridled speech: ' There is nothing men like better than wasting their time talking about things that do not concern them, and taking away people's characters. The community where these things are not avoided is in a dangerous condition.'[13] And again: ' We should use the gift of speech for the edification of our neighbour, for whom Our Lord shed His holy Blood, rather than for the injury of those who are absent, remembering that we will have to render an account for every idle word.'[14] He quotes for them the words of St. Paul to the Galatians: ' If you bite and devour one another, take heed you be not consumed one of another.'[15]

At the end of this section of the rule, St. Columban has some general observations on life in a monastery. In a monastery monks live in the company of others, that from one they may learn humility, from another patience, from another proper use of the tongue, from another gentleness. They live under the rule of a superior, following his will, not their own. They go to bed tired; they rise still heavy with sleep. When they suffer injury they are silent. Let them fear their superior as a master; let them love him as a father.

The rule was hard, undoubtedly, and St. Columban knew that. But of its success there can be no doubt. He could not but have seen how Heaven was blessing his work, as the love of God grew in the hearts of those around him and led them far on the road to sanctity. Of those who lived with him in Luxeuil, at least seventeen are to-day honoured as saints; and for hundreds of years to come Luxeuil was recognised throughout France as the outstanding centre of sanctity and learning.

Chapter VII.

'AUDAX IN CAUSA VERITATIS.'

THE words of the Gospel that he preached every day were never far from the mind of Columban, and he was not taken unawares when they were fulfilled in his regard. Clouds began to gather over the peaceful life in Luxeuil, and the prophetic words of Our Lord came vividly before him: 'You shall stand before governors and kings for My sake, for a testimony unto them.' The immorality of the court of Burgundy was a public scandal, and the zeal of St. Columban would not allow him be silent.

King Theoderic had left his lawful wife for other women; but, when St. Columban remonstrated with him, he at first promised amendment and declared himself willing to go back to his lawful wife. But his grandmother, Brunichild, the widow of Columban's first friend, Sigibert, was afraid that the lawful wife would take over the honours that she had usurped, and aroused Theoderic against Columban. One day, when Columban was at the royal court at Bruyeres-le-Chatel, near Paris, Brunichild brought the illegitimate sons of Theoderic to Columban for his blessing.

'What do they want?' said Columban.

'They are the king's sons; give them your blessing.'

'I would have you know that they shall never rule, for they are illegitimate.'

Brunichild flew into a rage, and sent the children away. As Columban was leaving the palace, the whole house shook, striking terror into all. But the anger of Brunichild was not lessened, and she began to lay her plans. She sent word to the king's men in Luxeuil that no one was to be allowed leave the monastery, no food was to be given to the monks, and no one was to receive them into their homes.

Columban heard of the orders that had been given and hastened back to Luxeuil. On his way he came to the royal palace at Epoisses, where Theoderic himself happened to be at the time. Word was sent to the king that Columban had come, but that he refused to enter the palace. 'Theoderic thought it would be wiser to pay due honour to the man of God, rather than to provoke the anger of God by insulting His servants. He, therefore, ordered a royal feast to be prepared and sent to Columban. When he saw the royal dishes, he asked what did this mean. On being told that the king had sent them, he refused to touch them, saying: " It is written: ' The Most High approveth not the gifts of the wicked.'[16] It is not fitting that the lips of the servants of God should be defiled by the food of him who denies them entry, not only to their own home, but even to the homes of others." At these words, the goblets were all smashed, the wine and the other drinks flowed out on the ground, and the rest of the food was scattered. When the terrified servants told the king what had happened, he was struck with fear, and he and his grandmother, Brunichild, hastened to Columban to ask his pardon and promised amendment. Satisfied with these promises, Columban returned to Luxeuil.

' But they did not keep their promises long. On the contrary, their transgressions increased, and Theoderic continued his irregular alliances. Columban heard of their relapse, and sent them a stinging letter, threatening them with excommunication if they did not amend. Brunichild again set about rousing the king against Columban, and enlisted the help of the courtiers and the nobles. She also approached the bishops, attack-

ing the mode of life in Luxeuil and the rule that
Columban had imposed on his monks.'

The move to bring the bishops into the fight was a
shrewd one. Brunichild knew her men. Many of them
were venal minions, who were always ready to fight
her cause; they were all the more willing, when the
enemy was one whose life was a constant rebuke to
their worldliness and whose zeal would not spare them.
They could not openly attack him for his denunciation
of the immorality of the court; their attack should
have at least the semblance of justification.

When Columban and his friends settled down in
Burgundy they naturally continued to observe the
customs that they had known in Ireland. Those who
joined them in Annegray and Luxeuil, all natives of
Gaul, easily fell into line; and, as the years went on
and their veneration for Columban grew, these men
became more and more attached to the customs of their
founder; not because those customs were Irish, but
simply because they were St. Columban's: Dominicans
or Franciscans do not look on the customs of their
founders as Spanish or Italian. The vast majority of
those who are sometimes charged with being too
tenacious of the customs of St. Columban were not
Irish but Gauls. Thus a diversity of customs arose,
that gave a pretext to those who wished to make
trouble, a pretext which the court-bishops were quick
to grasp. Their main attack centred around the date
for the celebration of Easter.

From the earliest times there had been considerable
diversity on this question in all parts of the Church,
and new methods of computation were being frequently
introduced. The Irish had continued to use a cycle
that had been dropped in Rome. The new Roman
cycle had been introduced into Gaul, and thus it
happened that some years Columban and his monks
were celebrating Easter at a different date from the

rest of Gaul. This gave rise to a good deal of comment and criticism, and the bishops convened a synod to deal with the matter.

St. Columban did not attend the synod, but sent a long letter in which, while defending his own method of computation, he pleads with the bishops that they allow him and his followers to remain among them as friends. 'Diversity of customs has done great harm to the Church; but if we overcome the spirit of envy and pride we can live together in true charity. . . . Surely there should be room in Gaul for you and us, as there will be in heaven, if we are worthy. . . . Do you select whatever you think best, and follow it. . . . My one request is that you allow us to remain in peace here in the woods, where lie the bones of our seventeen brothers who have died. . . . I feel, too, that we, who have adopted a more strict form of life, should be defended by you, and not attacked. . . . You have your duties, we have ours; let us all follow Christ, our Head, in peace and charity. . . . We are all members of one Body, whether we are Gauls or Britons or Spaniards or of any other nationality. Let us, therefore, be united in prayer and mutual help, that we may all be united in glory.'

On this subject St. Columban wrote two letters to the Popes: one to St. Gregory the Great, the other to Pope Sabinian. From the contents and the tone of his letter to St. Gregory it is evident that it was meant to be a personal letter to the Pope, rather than a solemn appeal. He first puts the case for the Irish computation as strongly as he can, and encloses three treatises on the subject. He makes a vigorous attack on the contention of the bishops of Gaul, that Easter should not be celebrated with the Jews: 'What has that to do with case? Why should they be considered?' He appeals to the Pope to use his authority in quelling the storm that is raging around him.

He then asks what should be his attitude towards bishops who have received consecration through simony, or who have been living in a manner unworthy of their state: should he have any intercourse with them? Also, what about monks who, without their abbot's permission, have left their monasteries?

' I had hoped to discuss these and other matters with you personally; but bodily infirmity and the cares of my office have tied me down at home and have prevented me from drinking of the living fount of spiritual knowledge. . . . If I go, it will not be to see the glories of Rome, but to see you and to reverence the relics of the saints. I have read your book on the Pastoral Office; I liked it well; it is concise and full of sound inspiring thoughts. I hear that you have written two short books on the prophet Ezechiel; would you kindly send them to me, as I am most anxious to read them. I have read St. Jerome's six books on that prophet; but he does not cover half the ground. At least send me the second book, and the Commentary on the Canticles of Canticles, from the verse: ' I will go to the mountain of myrrh ' (4, 16) to the end. Might I suggest, too, that you write a commentary on Zachary. I know that I am asking much, but you have much to give. . . . I hope you will pardon the boldness with which I have written, and say at least one prayer to Our Lord for me.'

His letter to Pope Sabinian is much shorter, and deals only with the Easter question, and refers the Pope to his previous letter to St. Gregory. He complains that the bishops will not listen to any arguments; and asks that, *if no question of faith is involved,* they be permitted to observe Easter according to their own computation. He reminds the Pope, as St. Ireneus had reminded Pope Victor in identical circumstances, that St. Polycarp and Pope Anicetus had continued to be friends, without yielding on this very same subject.

In this question of the Easter controversy, it is well to remember that even at the present day the Church sanctions the celebration of Easter on different dates, sometimes even in the same city. Whether it coincides or not with the Jewish Passover is not considered.

It would seem that his letter to Pope St. Gregory never reached Rome. We do not know whether his letter to Pope Sabinian reached its destination or not. St. Columban continued to observe Easter according to his own system as long as he was in Luxeuil. Later his successors conformed to the Roman usage.

Chapter VIII.

' FORTIS IN TRIBULATIONIBUS.'

NOW the fight was joined. On the one side were the king, whose sins had been publicly denounced and the end of whose kingdom had been foretold; the queen-mother, whose ambitions had been thwarted; the courtiers, whose only interest was their own advancement; most, but not all, of the bishops, whose readiness to obey their royal masters had lately been shown by their banishment of their fellow-bishop, St. Didier of Vienne, who was later murdered. On the other side were St. Columban and his monks, as helpless as St. John the Baptist before Herod.

' The king went to Luxeuil and questioned Columban about the innovations that he had introduced, and asked why some parts of the monastery were not open to all. Columban replied with vigour and courage: it was not his custom to allow outsiders and people of the world to enter the living quarters of the monks; suitable accommodation had been provided for guests. The king answered that, if he wished to continue to benefit by his generosity, he should give free access to all parts of the monastery. Columban replied:

" If you attempt to violate what has been set up here by the bonds of discipline, I will never accept either your gifts or your support; and if you have come here to destroy the home of the servants of God and to subvert discipline, know that your kingdom will totter to the ground, and you and your whole race overthrown." A prophecy that was later fulfilled.'

' The king had been rash enough to enter the refectory; but, terrified at the words of Columban, he

44

hastily left. As Columban continued to upbraid him,
Theoderic replied: " I suppose that you hope to gain
the crown of martyrdom through me! I am not so
foolish as to perpetrate such a crime. I have a better
plan, by which those who wish to cut themselves off
from the world can return to where they came from."
The courtiers, also, made it known that they would
not have among them those who would not associate
with others. To all this Columban replied that he
would not leave the monastery, unless he was dragged
from it by force. The king then withdrew, but left
behind one of the nobles, a man named Baudulf, who
took Columban by force and led him away to
Besançon, there to await the decision of the king.'

Some of the monks were allowed to accompany him
to Besançon, where they were not under very strict
guard and could move freely through the town. One
day Columban heard that there were some men in the
prison, condemned to death. ' He went to the prison,
nobody standing in his way, and spoke to the men.
They promised him that if they were set free they
would amend their lives and would do penance for
their sins. Columban ordered Domualis—the same for
whom the water had come miraculously from the rock
in the early days in Annegray—to pull at the iron by
which the fetters were fastened. He did so, and it
came away like a rotten twig. Columban then loosed
their fetters, spoke to them again, and, following the
Gospel, washed their feet and dried them with a towel.
He told them to leave the prison and go to the church,
there to expiate their sins with tears of repentance.
When they reached the church they found the doors
locked against them. In the meantime, the tribune of
the soldiers had recovered from the shock of seeing
the hand of Heaven in the broken fetters and the
empty prison, and collected the soldiers to go in pursuit
of the fugitives. When they saw the soldiers coming

and the doors closed against them, they implored Columban to save them. He raised his eyes to Heaven and prayed God not to allow those whom He had just now set free to fall again into the hands of the guards. His prayer is heard; the strong locks of the church are opened, and the fugitives rush in; behind them the doors are again locked against the soldiers, as if some doorkeeper had unlocked them and then locked them again with a key. The tribune and his soldiers arrive at the church just as Columban and his monks reach it. They found the doors locked and sent for the sexton—his name was Aspasius—to get the key from him. He came and tried to open the doors, but remarked that he had never found them so firmly locked. After that no one dared molest those whom Providence had set free.'

Their stay at Besançon was made as comfortable as possible by the bishop of the diocese, St. Nicetius, who was an old friend of St. Columban. After the incident at the prison the guards saw that God was with him, and were not inclined to interfere. One Sunday morning he went to the top of one of the high hills that surround the city to see whether the road to Luxeuil was being guarded against him. He could see no one on guard, and so decided to leave. He called the others who had come with him from Luxeuil, and together they returned home.

In the meantime, the monks in Luxeuil had been trying to get from the king some relaxation of the restrictions on their movements. As their spokesman they sent Agilus, whose father had befriended Columban and whose mother was a cousin of the king. It is said that they were granted some relief; but the unauthorized return of Columban to Luxeuil again aroused the anger of the court. A posse of soldiers was immediately sent to Luxeuil, with orders to conduct him back to Besançon. Jonas describes what

happened: ' The soldiers arrived at the monastery and
began their search for Columban, who happened to
be sitting in the porch of the church, reading. More
than once they passed quite close to him, so close that
their feet touched his, and they rubbed against his
garments; and yet they could not see him. The
tribune, coming to a window, saw Columban sitting
down reading, unmolested, though the soldiers were
everywhere around him. He recognised the hand of
God and said to his men: " Why are you searching the
porch so carefully? That is useless. Don't deceive
yourselves; you cannot find what God has hidden. Let
us go to the king and tell him that you could not find
him." From this it is clear that the tribune did not
wish to injure Columban, and therefore had been
permitted to see him.'

The king received their report, and determined to
end the matter once and for all. He sent another posse
with strict orders to find him, and not to leave him
until they had conducted him beyond the confines of
the kingdom. The soldiers arrived at the monastery
when Columban and the monks were at Office. The
captain approached Columban and said to him: " Man
of God, we ask you to do as the king and as we command. Leave this place and go back by the same road
as you came by." Columban replied: " I do not
think that God would be pleased if a man were to
return to the native land that he had left for the sake
of Christ." The captain saw that his efforts were useless and left the monastery; but ordered a certain
number, noted for their determination, to remain and
carry out his orders. These men implored Columban
to have pity on them: they were the unlucky ones
who had been selected for this business; if they did
not remove him, even by force, their lives would be
in danger. But he replied that he had declared more
than once that he would not leave except by force.

They saw that they were in a great predicament and fell on their knees before him, begging him, with tears in their eyes, not to blame them for this great crime: they were not acting of their own will, but were only carrying out the orders of the king. He saw then that others would be in danger if the soldiers used force, and decided to leave.

As he was leaving the monastery, a sad group followed him, as if to his funeral. His heart was broken at the thought of being separated from so many who had entrusted their lives to him, and he raised his eyes to Heaven and prayed: " O Eternal Creator, prepare a place for us, where Thy servants may serve Thee for ever." He told his monks not to lose hope, but to continue to praise God without ceasing: what had happened would not be to his or to their loss, but would result in a greater increase in the number of monasteries. Whoever might wish to follow him, should come with a firm determination to share in his hardships; those who wished to remain in Luxeuil could do so with perfect freedom and an easy conscience. The Lord would soon take vengeance for their sufferings.

All declared their readiness to follow him and share in his sufferings; but the guards told them that the king's orders were that none were to go with him, except those who were natives of Ireland or Britain; those who were natives of Gaul were to remain in Luxeuil. That was the hardest blow of all. National distinctions had never meant anything to St. Columban. As he had written to the bishops of Gaul: " We are all members of one Body, whether Gauls or Britons or Spaniards or natives of any other country." The vast majority of his monks were natives of Gaul. The men on whom he relied most were Burgundians: Attala, whom he recommended as superior of Luxeuil and who was to succeed him in Bobbio; Eustasius,

who later succeeded him in Luxeuil; Waldalenus, his
second choice for Luxeuil: all natives of Burgundy.
Many others, like Donatus and Agilus, had been under
his care from their childhood. It was hard to leave
them all. When he first saw Luxeuil, it was a ruin. In
the twenty years that had elapsed he had seen the town
grow up around his monastery and the people had
taken him to their hearts, as their descendants have
done to the present day. He had been happy in
Luxeuil, happy especially at the consolation that
Heaven had sent him, of seeing so many of his friends
far advanced on the road to heroic sanctity. Nor could
he forget those who were sleeping their last sleep
nearby, with the saintly companion of all his wanderings, the younger Columban.

The king's orders were ruthlessly carried out, and
Columban and his friends were dragged from their
home to begin their long road to exile. Their destination was the city of Nantes, on the west coast of
France; but for many reasons the route they took was
not the direct one. They first went south towards
Besançon, and they were not long on the road when
one of their number, Deicola, who had come from
Bangor with Columban, found his strength failing and
asked permission to remain behind. The permission
was granted, and Deicola remained in the ' desert '
and ultimately founded the important abbey of Lure,
about twelve miles south of Luxeuil.

From Besançon their route went through Chalons-
sur-Saone, Autun, Avallon, Auxerre and on to Nevers
on the river Loire, where they were to take boat for
Nantes. ' Because they were somewhat slow in getting
aboard the boat, one of the guards seized an oar and
struck one of the monks, named Lua, a most saintly
man. Columban saw the blow and cried out: " You
cruel wretch, why do you add sorrow to sorrow? Have
you not done enough already to bring ruin upon your-

D

.self? Why are you harsh to those who are meek and vicious to the gentle? Remember, the vengeance of Heaven will strike you at this same spot, where in your madness you struck one of Christ's members.'' The retribution that soon followed put the seal of approval on the sentence; for, on his return journey, as he was crossing the river at this same place, he fell in and was drowned.'

Their next stop was at Orleans, where, by orders of the king, all the churches were closed against them, and they were obliged to take their rest in tents on the banks of the Loire. Their supplies were running short and they sent two of their number into the city for food. One of them was Potentinus, who, Jonas tells us, was still alive when he wrote, and had founded a monastery near Coutances, in Armorica. They went through the whole city, but got nothing: all were afraid to disobey the king's orders. As they were leaving the city they met a Syrian woman, who asked them who they were. They told her who they were and that they had been looking for supplies, but could not get any. '' Come to my lodgings,'' she said, '' and take what you need. I, too, am a stranger from the far-off Orient.'' They gladly followed her to her lodgings, and there saw her husband, who was blind. When they asked her who he was, she replied: '' He is my husband; also a Syrian. He has been blind for many years, and I lead him around.'' They told her that if she brought him to the servant of God, Columban, perhaps his prayers could restore her husband's sight. The faith of the blind man was aroused and, with his wife leading him, he followed the monks to the boat. Potentinus told Columban of the kind hospitality that they had received, and the blind man implored him to pray for him, that his sight might be restored. Seeing his faith, Columban asked all to pray for him. He himself fell on his knees and remained for a long time in prayer; then he arose, made the Sign of the Cross on the man's eyes and his sight was restored. In Orleans, too, he cured many who were possessed by the devil. Moved by such evidence of Divine intervention, the people of the city began to honour Columban; but they could not help him openly, for they feared the guards and the anger of the king.

They continued their journey down the Loire and came to the city of Tours, where Columban asked them to allow him visit the tomb of St. Martin. Those in charge refused, and told the sailors to keep to the centre of the river and to row fast. Columban heard these orders and raised his eyes to Heaven in prayer, complaining that he was not even allowed visit the tombs of the saints. When they came opposite the city, though the sailors were rowing with all their might, the boat slowed down and headed for the shore. The guards saw that their efforts were useless, and allowed the boat to take its course. Columban landed and went to the tomb of St. Martin, where he spent the night in prayer.

Next day he was invited by Leuparius, the bishop of the city, to partake of his hospitality; he accepted and remained with the bishop that day. While they were at table the bishop asked Columban why he was returning to his native land. Columban replied: "That dog Theoderic has driven me from my friends." Then one of the guests, who was a follower of Theoderic, said in a low voice that it was better to drink milk than wormwood. "I see," said Columban, "that you mean to remain loyal to Theoderic." The other admitted that he would keep his oath of loyalty as long as he could. "In that case," said Columban, "you will be glad to bring him a message from me. Tell him that within three years he and his children will perish, and that his whole family will be uprooted

D2

by God." "Why do you say that?" "When God bids me speak I cannot be silent." Jonas adds: 'All the people of Gaul have seen this prophecy fulfilled.'

Columban returned to the boat to find his friends utterly dejected: all their money had been stolen, even the little they had left after they had given alms to the poor. He went back at once to the tomb of St. Martin and 'complained that he should not have allowed his friends to be robbed while he was visiting his tomb. Soon the man who had taken the money was heard to groan in pain, and he told where the money was hidden. His companions also returned what they had taken, and asked Columban to forgive them. After that none dare take anything belonging to the man of God.' The bishop was very kind to them and gave them all they needed.

They continued their journey and arrived at Nantes, where they were to take ship for Ireland. There was, of course, no regular service, and they had to sit down and wait. The bishop of the city was not at all friendly; not only would he not give them anything, but he would not even sell them what they needed. The people, however, were friendly.

One day a poor man came to where they were staying, asking for help. Columban called the monk who was acting as bursar, and told him to give the man something to eat.

"We have no bread, and only a little meal."

"How much have you?" said Columban.

"Not more than one measure, I think."

"Give him what you have; don't worry about to-morrow."

The bursar gave all they had to the poor man and kept nothing for themselves. For the next three days they went hungry. On the third day there was a knock at the door. A man had come from a woman named Procula, who said that she had been inspired by God

' to send help to a servant of God named Columban
and his friends, who were living in Nantes.' The
supplies would come next day, and the man had come
beforehand to tell them to have the necessary con-
tainers ready. There would be one hundred measures
of wine, two hundred measures of corn and one
hundred measures of malt. Columban summoned them
all together, to pray for their benefactor and to thank
God for His goodness to them. ' How wonderful is the
love of God! He allows us to be in want, that He may
show His love in relieving us; He allows us to be
tempted, that our hearts may be drawn ever closer to
His protecting love; He permits His members to be
sorely tried, that their love for the Divine Healer may
be increased!'

While they were waiting for the ship, Columban
took the opportunity of writing to those left behind
in Luxeuil.

Chapter IX.

'WHEREVER THE WAY OF SALVATION MIGHT LEAD.'

DURING their enforced stay in Nantes, Columban and his friends had won the hearts of the people, who made no secret of their sympathy, giving them whatever food they needed and showing them every kindness. This the bishop did not like; it showed up his own want of hospitality in too dark colours; and he joined with the captain of the soldiers in urging Columban to get a ship and leave. Columban replied:

" If there is a boat sailing for Ireland, put all our belongings on board, and let my companions go on board. I will take a small boat on the Loire as far as the open sea."

To this they agreed. As Columban suspected, they were only too anxious to be rid of him. A cargo boat trading with Ireland was found, and his companions went on board, with all their belongings. As the ship was sailing for the open sea, a storm arose and they were driven high and dry on the shore, where they stuck fast for three days. The captain of the ship decided that he had had enough trouble from Columban and his friends, and sailed away as soon as the ship floated. By this time the guard that had come from Luxeuil had eagerly taken the opportunity to start for home; and the bishop did not dare run counter to the feelings of the people, who vied with one another in honouring and helping them. They were now free from all restraint.

Columban had now to decide where they would settle down. All France was in hostile hands, with the exception of the small kingdom of Neustria, on the north coast, where the king, Clothaire, was friendly. He had often expressed the desire to go to Rome, not to see the glories of the ancient city, but to see the Pope, and to venerate the relics of the saints. That wish must have strongly influenced the decision he now took, to cross the Alps and go into Italy. It was to be a long and tedious journey, lasting more than three years; but it was destined to prove, in a very extraordinary manner, the truth of his prophecy to his monks on leaving Luxeuil, that from their banishment would come a great increase in the number of monasteries.

For his journey through France he naturally avoided the territory of his enemy, Theoderic, and took the shortest route to the kingdom of Neustria, where he knew he could rely on a friendly reception from Clothaire, who would also afford him protection for the rest of his journey. It was probably at Rouen that he met the king, who urged him to settle down in his territory. Columban, as we know, had different plans; but he so far acceded to the wishes of the king as to stay for some time at the royal court. During his visit he did not hesitate to reprimand the king for what Jonas calls the usual sins of royal courts. Clothaire took the reprimands well and promised amendment.

This visit brought many a blessing to the house of Clothaire, who, in a few years, was to rule practically all France; and recalls to mind the words of Jonas that ' in whatever house he stayed, he drew all to the service of God.' During the reign of Dagobert, son and successor of Clothaire, the court was more like a monastery than a kingly palace, especially after the arrival there of the great St. Eloi. Dagobert's son and successor, Sigibert, is a canonized saint. His son, Dagobert II, should have succeeded, but was put aside by the mayor of the palace and fled to Ireland. (An ancient tradition speaks of two French princes living in Slane.) He subsequently returned to France, where he was murdered in a conspiracy. He, too, is honoured as a saint. At least twenty saints can be counted who were at one time or another connected with the courts of these kings.

While Columban was in Neustria, a dispute arose about boundaries between Theodebert and Theoderic, and both sent representatives to Clothaire to ask for help. Clothaire put the matter before Columban and asked his advice. He replied: "Do not take sides; within three years both kingdoms will be yours." Clothaire accepted the advice and remained neutral.

Clothaire provided them with an escort for their journey through Austrasia. Their way led through Paris, at the gates of which Columban cured a man possessed by the devil. From Paris they went to Meaux, where they stayed at the home of a nobleman, named Chagneric, who gave them a very hearty welcome. He told them to send back the escort: he would give them all the help and protection they would need. Jonas tells us that ' he dispensed with the help of others, that he might keep Columban with him as long as possible, that his home might be blessed by his teaching.' Columban remained with him for a short time, and blessed his home and his children, a son named Faron and an infant daughter named Fara. The elder son, Chagnauld, was probably a monk in Luxeuil at this time. As we shall see, this visit, too, was very fruitful in the increase of monasteries.

From Meaux they went on to Ussy-sur-Marne, where they were received by a man named Autherius and his wife Aiga, who brought their young sons to be blessed by Columban. Their names were Ado, Ouen (Audoen) and Radon. Jonas immediately adds: ' So abundantly did the grace of God fill his soul, that whomsoever he blessed continued in the practice of virtue until death.' His words were certainly true in this case. Ado was the founder of the monastery of Jouarre. Audoen became archbishop of Rouen, and, in co-operation with St. Eloi, founded many monasteries in that part of France.[37] Columban stayed in that town for some time, going about among the people, warning the wayward to amend their lives.

Their next stop was at the court of Theodebert, king of Austrasia, at Metz, where they had the happiness of meeting again some of the friends from Luxeuil. In his letter from Nantes, Columban had told them that they were free to remain in Luxeuil or to follow him; but he warned them that they should not follow him for any affection they might have for him, but only if they felt it would be for their spiritual good. They had heard of his progress through France, and some of them set out to intercept him at Metz. We do not know who they all were, but Attala, Eustasius and Chagnoald were among them. The king had received them very cordially and urged Columban to remain in his territory, pointing out to him that he could easily find a suitable place from which to preach to the neighbouring peoples. Columban agreed to remain for some time in his territory, and selected a place called Bregenz, away at the extreme south-east corner of Austrasia, on Lake Constance. He was probably influenced in his selection by the fact that Bregenz would be a convenient base from which to work among the pagans to the east; and also because it was very near his ultimate objective.

The king gave them an escort and they went down the river Moselle to Coblenz, where it joins the Rhine. On their journey up the Rhine, their supplies began to fail when they were near the city of Mainz. The sailors said that they had some friends in the city who would help them. They went to their friends, and came back empty-handed. "Now," said Columban, "let me go to my Friend." They knew he had never been in the city before and could not possibly know anyone there. He, however, went to the church and fell on his knees in prayer. He had been some time praying when the bishop of the place, whose name was Lesio, happened to come from his house to the church. He saw the man praying and asked him who he was.

' I am a stranger on a journey,' said Columban.

' If you need anything,' said the bishop, ' come to my house and take whatever you need.' Columban told him that he had others with him, who were waiting at the bank of the river. The bishop sent his servant to tell them to leave one on guard and the rest to come and take what they needed. The bishop never forgot the incident; and, when telling about it afterwards, he used to say that never before had he felt so clearly inspired to give help, and that his visit to the church at that particular time was due to nothing but the intervention of Providence on behalf of the blessed Columban.

It was probably on this journey that St. Columban composed his Boat Song, the Carmen Navale. Here are the first and last verses:

En silvis caesa fluctu meat acta carina
Bicornis Rheni, et pelagus perlabitur uncta.
Heia viri! nostrum reboans echo sonet heia.

***   ***   ***   ***

Rex quoque virtutum rerum fons summa potestas
Certanti spondet, vincenti praemia donat.
Vestra, viri, Christum memorans personet heia! [38]

Chapter X.

IN SWITZERLAND.

THEY continued their journey up the Rhine, into what is now Switzerland, then inhabited by the Alemanni. That German tribe had overrun the settlements that the Romans had made, and had, in its turn, been conquered by the Franks. Even in Roman times they had retained their own laws and their pagan worship; after their defeat by the Franks they had not followed their conquerors into the Church. Scattered throughout the country there remained a few Catholic communities from Roman times; these and the silent blessing of many a ruined church gave the monks some hope of success.

They left the Rhine at the point where the river from Lake Zurich enters it. Tradition says that at this point St. Ursicinus left them, to found his own monastery and, consequently, the town of St. Ursanne, on the French-Swiss border. He is said to have been one of the original twelve who had come from Ireland. On the shores of Lake Zurich they stopped at a small place called Tuconia, now Tuggen, where the people were entirely pagan, and still continued the worship of idols and all manner of superstition. Even the few Christians that had remained had lapsed into the idolatry of their neighbours. Columban and his friends did what they could to convert them, but met with little success. The Life of St. Gall tells that he set fire to the temples and threw the sacrificial offerings into the lake. Serious threats were uttered against them, and they shook the dust from their feet and left.

59

They then went east towards Lake Constance. On the shore of that lake they came to the town of Arbon, which was a Christian oasis in the desert of paganism, where the priest, Willimar, received them very hospitably and kept them with him for a week, giving them all the information on the character and customs of the people. Columban asked him if he knew any place that would be suitable for a monastery. ' Yes,' he said, ' on the other side of the lake are the ruins of an old settlement, on a large plain at the foot of the mountain. The soil is good and could easily be cultivated.' They decided to have a look at it, and got a small boat to cross the lake. The place did not appeal to them very much, but, as there was a pagan tribe of the Suevi living nearby, Columban was induced to settle down there: he might be able to bring some into the Church.

They soon had an additional incentive to their zeal. In the district they came across a church that had been dedicated in honour of St. Aurelia, now turned into a pagan temple, with the idols of the gods and the other paraphernalia of pagan worship. The language was, of course, a great difficulty; but, according to the Life of St. Gall, ' Gall had received this favour from God that he had no small knowledge of the native dialect as well as of Latin '; and he was commissioned to preach by Columban. On one of the great days for pagan worship, a great crowd had gathered for the ceremonies, and to see the strangers who had come. When they were all assembled, Gall began to preach, exhorting them to cast aside their pagan superstitions and to turn to the Lord. Then he broke the idols and threw them into the lake. Some, probably of those who had been Catholics, were converted and confessed their sins; the others were roused to indignation at the destruction of their idols, and determined to drive the invaders out.

It would seem that at no time did Columban intend to settle down permanently in Bregenz. He had acceded to the request of Theodebert to remain for some time in his territories, especially when it had been pointed out to him that he and his friends would have an opportunity of preaching the Gospel to the neighbouring pagan peoples. The immediate surroundings of Bregenz did not, apparently, please them well; but this, their first chance to attack organized paganism, could not be refused. So they remained there for more than two years, following their daily horarium of prayer and work, and continuing to preach the Gospel, in spite of the continued opposition of the pagan priests, who had succeeded in winning over to their side the local representative of King Theodebert. Though not without fruit, it was hard and discouraging work. The foundation in Bregenz was not intended to be permanent; and yet, on that same site the monastic life has continued, practically unbroken, down to the present day: it is now the Cistercian Abbey of Mehrerau.

In the meantime, the war that had so long threatened between the two brothers, Theodebert and Theoderic, had broken out; and Columban sent advice to his benefactor, Theodebert, to give up his royal status and enter a monastery: he should not run the risk of losing his eternal kingdom along with his earthly one. ' But the king and all his court laughed him to scorn: whoever heard of a Merovingian ruler becoming a cleric against his will! ' Columban replied with the warning: ' If he does not become a cleric now of his own free will, in a short time he will be a cleric against his will.' The warning was in vain and the war went on. The decisive battle was fought at Zulpich, near Cologne, where Theodebert was utterly defeated and thousands of his army were slain. He himself escaped for a while, but was ultimately captured, and forced into a monastery; a short time later he was put to death. 'At the time the battle was being fought at Zulpich, Columban was alone in the desert with Chagnoald, sitting on the trunk of an old tree, reading. Suddenly a kind of drowsiness came over him and he had a vision of what was happening. When he awoke, he told Chagnoald of the battle, and lamented that so much blood was being spilt. Chagnoald ventured to say:

'Father, help Theodebert by your prayers, that he may conquer Theoderic, who is our enemy.'

Columban replied:

'Your advice is not good; it is contrary to sound religion. Our Lord has told us that we should pray for our enemies. The fate of these men is in the hands of the just Judge.'

As a result of the battle of Zulpich the whole country around Bregenz fell into the hands of Theoderic, the same who had banished Columban from Luxeuil, and it became impossible for them to remain any longer in that neighbourhood. Columban was inclined to go east, into the country of the Veneti, a Slav people; but a strange vision made him change his plan. 'An angel of God appeared to him and, in a small circle such as is made with a style, showed him the whole world. 'Here,' said the angel, 'you see the whole world; go to the right or to the left, that you may enjoy the fruits of your labours.' However we may interpret this, Columban understood from it that the Veneti were not yet ready to receive the faith. He therefore decided to go into Italy, as seems to have been his original intention, and, if possible, to see the Pope in Rome.

It is at this point that the Lives of St. Gall tell of the incident that caused the separation between him and St. Columban. As the story goes, Gall fell sick at the moment of departure, and asked permission to remain behind. Columban thought that Gall wished to remain behind because he was attached too much to Bregenz, and because he had not the courage to face the troubles of an uncertain future. He reluctantly gave the permission, but forbade him to say Mass as long as he (Columban) was alive. A few years later, very early on a Sunday morning, when the monks had returned to their cells after Matins, Gall called his deacon, Magnoaldus, and told him to prepare the vestments for Mass. ' Are you going to say Mass yourself?' asked Magnoaldus. Gall replied: ' I have learned in a vision that my lord and father Columban has this day passed from the miseries of this life to the joys of Paradise; and therefore I must say Mass for the repose of his soul.' After Mass, Gall told Magnoaldus to go to Bobbio 'and make diligent inquiry about my abbot; and if you find that he has died, note well the day and the hour, that you may know if there be truth in my vision.' Magnoaldus went to Bobbio, and found out that all had happened as had been revealed to Gall. The monks of Bobbio gave him a letter giving the account of the death of St. Columban, and also his *cambutta,* or pastoral staff, by which Gall might know that he was again free to say Mass. When Gall read the letter he wept bitterly, for he had a great affection for his master; and ' they continued to offer prayers and Masses in memory of that sainted father.'

There are many reasons against accepting this story. The Lives of St. Gall which tell of it are at least one hundred and fifty years after the event. Jonas is silent about it, though he often spoke to Gall about St. Columban; and much of this story is laid in Jonas' own abbey of Bobbio. If we accept the story, we must accept it in its entirety, and find in it a proof of the extraordinary hold that St. Columban had on his followers, whose respect and affection for him could not be shaken even by what seemed to be very harsh treatment. St. Gall's affection for his master continued to be reflected in the traditions of his abbey, and the city of his name has retained it to the present day.

Chapter XI.

IN THE COURT OF THE LOMBARDS.

ST. COLUMBAN had now come to the final stage in his long journey, which was to bring him to his last resting place on earth. Very few of his companions on that journey were now with him. That, however, did not surprise him: he had foretold that the banishment from Luxeuil was destined to result in a great increase in the number of monasteries, and thus deprive him of many of his oldest friends. Very early in the journey, St. Deicola had stopped at Lure; Potentinus had gone to Armorica to found Coutances; St. Ursicinus had turned aside to found St. Ursanne; if the legend can be relied on, St. Sigibert had left Bregenz to establish the monastery of Dissentis in Switzerland; St. Eustasius and St. Chagnoald had been sent back by St. Columban to Luxeuil, the former to be abbot there, the latter to be ultimately the bishop of Laon, and to assist his sister, St. Fara, in the foundation of her monastery of Faremoutiers. St. Gall and St. Magnus were now staying in Bregenz, to lay the foundations on which the monastery of St. Gall was later built. Of those whose names have come down to us, only St. Attala, his favourite, was now with him. We know, however, from the accounts of the foundation of Bobbio, that many from his earlier monasteries had availed themselves of his permission to follow him. Their route lay due south to Milan, where Agiluph, the king of the Lombards, had his court at the time. There Columban was faced with a very complex situation.

65

E

The Lombards, who at that time were in control of northern Italy, had received Christianity from the Arians, and political considerations had made them tenacious of their heresy long after the intellectual dispute was elsewhere dead. The king, though an Arian, was not antagonistic to the Church, and had allowed his children to be baptised by Catholic priests. His queen, Theodelinda, a Bavarian princess, was a sincere Catholic, who was anxious to bring her erring subjects back to the unity of the faith. One very serious obstacle to the conversion of the Arians was the schism that had grown out of the Three Chapters dispute, and which still continued in northern Italy; the queen herself was at least sympathetic to the schismatics, and many friendly letters from St. Gregory the Great had not been able to change her attitude. They had both known Columban by repute, and gave him a very sincere welcome to their court, as one on whose help they could rely to settle their religious differences.

On his arrival Columban began to work for the conversion of the Arians, both by speech and pen. The sincerity of the queen and the sympathy of the king greatly encouraged his efforts; but he soon realised that the schism was a very formidable obstacle, which would have to be removed before there could be any hope of success. While it lasted, the road to the Church was befogged by such a cloud of suspicion and doubt converning the very centre of unity that no Arian could be expected to find his way. As St. Columban's action in this matter has often been severely criticised, it is necessary to say something about the origin and progress of this schism.

The history of the controversy of the Three Chapters is very confusing, the confusion beginning with the very terms employed. Some apply the words to certain writings of three bishops, Theodore of Mopsuestia,

Theodoret of Cyrus, and Ibas of Edessa, which had been attacked as being Nestorian; others mean by the Three Chapters the edict of the Emperor that condemned these writings. We will use it in the first sense.

The Council of Ephesus in 431 had condemned Nestorianism, which held that there were two persons in Christ. The Council of Chalcedon in 451 condemned the Monophysites, who held that there was only one nature in Christ. Theodore of Mopsuestia was accused of Nestorianism, but had died three years before the Council of Ephesus, in full communion with the Church. Theodoret and Ibas were also accused of being Nestorians, and had been driven from their sees by the Monophysites; but the Council of Chalcedon declared their orthodoxy and restored them to their sees. So things remained for about a hundred years, when the Emperor Justinian was persuaded by pro-Monophysite intriguers that the Monophysites would return to the Church if Theodore, Theodoret and Ibas were condemned. This the Emperor proceeded to do in an Edict, to which he demanded the signatures of the bishops. Reluctantly, under pressure of threats, the majority of the Eastern bishops signed; the Western bishops, with Pope Vigilius at their head, refused to sign. The bishops thought it improper to condemn men who had died so long ago, in full union with the Church; they especially resented the implied slur on the Council of Chalcedon, which had restored Theodoret and Ibas to their sees.

Justinian then struck at the head of the opposition, and summoned Pope Vigilius to Constantinople, where he was detained for nearly three years, until he consented to condemn the Three Chapters. This action aroused such a storm of opposition in the West that the Pope withdrew his condemnation. It was then agreed to submit the matter to a general Council, both sides to be silent in the meantime. Justinian broke his

E2

word, and the Pope withdrew his consent to the calling of a General Council, and was subjected to very harsh treatment, of which he complained to the whole world. The Council, however, was called by the Emperor in 553, the vast majority of the bishops being from the East. The Council condemned the Three Chapters, and Pope Vigilius, again refusing his consent, was banished. Ultimately, however, after much suffering, he approved the decrees of the Council, which took its place as the 5th Eucumenical Council, though it was many years before it was universally recognised as such. Vigilius died without returning to Rome. The decrees were later approved by Pelagius I, the successor of Vigilius, though he had been strongly opposed to the Emperor's action before he became Pope.

Again the bishops of the West, especially those in Africa and Italy, strongly objected. They felt that the Pope had, by implication, condemned the action of the Council of Chalcedon, yielding to the violence to which he had been subjected by the Emperor, whose chief instigators were those Monophysite heretics who had been condemned by Chalcedon. Many felt so strongly on the matter that they refused to hold any communication with Rome. Thus began the schism.

It is not hard to imagine how bewildered were the minds of the people in the West as contradictory reports began to arrive from Constantinople. They knew that Vigilius had gone to Constantinople firm in his intention to withstand the Emperor; but the accounts that came back greatly disturbed them. To the minds of the Western bishops the surrender by the Pope meant a victory for the Monophysite heretics; and as party feeling grew, the orthodoxy of the Pope himself began to come under suspicion. It was not. easy for the people of the West to get the true facts of the case, as they were ignorant of the Greek language, in which the proceedings of the Council were written; and when it was reported that the minutes of the Council had been tampered with, their doubts were more confounded. With the bishops so violently divided against the Pope, the ordinary man in the street must have been utterly bewildered.

The presence of the Arian heresy in northern Italy made the situation there more deplorable. Schism is always bad; but, when it constitutes a formidable obstacle to the return of heretics to the Church, it is doubly disastrous, and its removal imperative. The friendship that had grown up between Columban and the king, as proved by the royal donation of the lands of Bobbio, had given him well-founded hopes for success in his efforts to convert the Arians. But the schism was a stumbling block. How could an Arian, or any other heretic, submit to a Church that was suspect to so many of its members? Then the queen asked him to write to the Pope. But he was only a stranger, just lately arrived; and he held no official position in the Church. Others, too, asked him to write; and he still hesitated. Then the king asked him. That settled it. When an heretical king asked a stranger like him to write to the Pope to end the internal dissensions in the Church in his dominions, he could no longer refuse; and his well-founded hopes for the conversion of the Arians determined him to write as forcibly as possible.

The letter is a strong appeal that a synod be called, at which the true doctrine of the Incarnation would be publicly and solemnly proclaimed, so that from the Holy See may be removed the suspicion that it had patronized heretics, ' something which cannot be true, either in the past or at present or in the future.' He does not deal with the origin or progress of the schism; he never mentions the three bishops nor the Council of Chalcedon. With these things he was not concerned. His sole concern was the removal of the suspicion of heterodoxy from the Holy See. He felt that once the accretions of suspicion that had grown out of the schism had been cleared away, the *raison d'être* for the schism would be destroyed, and a very serious obstacle to the conversion of the Arians removed. He does not hesitate to call on the Pope, again and again, to do his duty. ' You are the true shepherd; speak to them with the voice of the true shepherd. You are the master and the helmsman of the spiritual bark; watch, for the seas are stormy. You are the commander-in-chief of the army; take your place in the front line to lead.' He asks pardon for speaking so boldly; but to an Irishman all forms of dissension or want of unity are distasteful: ' in our land there are no heretics, no schismatics, no Jews.' Nor should any question his devotion and attachment to the Holy See: ' we are bound *(devincti sumus)* to the Chair of Peter; Rome may be great and renowned: it is only through that Chair that she is illustrious in our eyes; the faith which we have received from you, the successors of the Apostles, we have kept unsullied.' The situation loudly calls for action, solemn and public. If that is not forthcoming, you cannot expect to be free from the judgments of your inferiors. ' Pardon me, Holy Father, if I seem to point out your duty to you. Your flock is running hither and thither, uncertain where to turn; do not remain silent, but let the voice of the true shepherd be heard, clear and unmistakable, that all Italy may follow you, the Rock of the King of Kings, that the fold of Christ may again be one.'

In this letter St. Columban was not concerned with the facts of the controversy; his only aim was to remove from the Holy See the suspicions that had arisen. He was in a strong position to have good hopes that, once the schism was ended, the Arian

king might bring his Arian subjects into the Church.
To refuse the request of the king, or to allow his due
reverence for the Holy See to minimise the urgency of
his appeal would lay him open to the charge of throw-
ing away the golden opportunity that Providence had
given him.

We do not know whether this letter ever reached
its destination; no reply has been discovered. The
schism and the heresy dragged on; and St. Columban
did not have the happiness of seeing success.
Agilulph's son and successor was a Catholic, but did
not reign long; his successor was a bigoted Arian. The
work of St. Columban was continued by his monks in
Bobbio, and was finally crowned with success. Jonas
gives us one incident in the struggle, which is interesting and instructive:

'One of the priests of Bobbio, named Blidulf, was
sent by the blessed Attala to the city of Pavia. One
day as he was walking through the city he met a
chief of the Lombards, named Ariowaldus, who
sneered when he saw the monk: "This is one of
Columban's monks, who will not return our salute."
When he was some distance away, he ironically saluted
Blidulf, who said to him: " I would gladly return your
salute, if you did not cling to false doctrines, and if
you did not favour those who are leading you astray;
you call these men priests, making a mockery of the
name. You should confess one God in the Blessed
Trinity; not three powers, but three persons; nor one
person under three names, but three persons in truth,
the Father and the Son and the Holy Ghost; one
power, one will, one essence." Ariowaldus went off,
asking was there no Arian who would waylay this
monk and beat him to death. Two of them volunteered
to do it, and one night attacked the priest, as he was
returning from a supper to which one of the Catholics
had invited him. They beat him on the head and on

every part of the body, and left him for dead. Meantime, the person with whom the priest was staying became alarmed when his friend was not returning, and, fearing that he might have fallen into the hands of the Arians, took his stick and set out to find him. He found him lying on the road, miraculously recovered from his experience. Shortly afterwards, the culprits confessed; but one of them later boasted of his crime, and died suddenly. ' He was buried at some distance from the other graves, but in a prominent place, that the passer-by might say: '' There lies the reprobate who attacked the monk from Bobbio.''

Chapter XII.

BOBBIO.

THE king had given him permission to settle down anywhere in his territory; and, during their stay in Milan, they were looking out for some suitable site. ' One day a man named Jocundus came to the king and told him that he knew of a place in the Apennines, where there was a basilica dedicated in honour of St. Peter, Prince of the Apostles; the land was fertile, well watered and good fishing. The old name of the place is Bobbio, from a river that flows near by.'

Columban went and looked at the place, and found it very suitable for a monastery. Perfect solitude, good building material in the woods, plenty of fish in the rivers Trebbia and Bobbio, and enough fertile land to satisfy their needs. The king, in a document that has come down to us, granted to St. Columban: ' the Basilica of the Blessed Prince of the Apostles, Peter, and all the land, whether cultivated or not, within four miles, with the exception of one half of the well, which we have already deeded to Sundrarit.' Donation of half a well will certainly sound strange to the modern reader; but stranger still is the fact that the well still exists, divided by the wall of the old abbey, the outer portion still in use for the people of Bobbio.

He tells us himself that he was now a weak old man:

    " . . . . morbis oppressus acerbis,

    " Corpore quos fragili patior, tristique senecta

    " Nunc ad Olympiadis ter senos venimus annos."[39]

So now we find Columban, now an old man nearly eighty years of age, if not more, setting out to restore

73

the ruined church of the Prince of the Apostles. It
was a hard task; but he had the great consolation of
having Attala with him, a man for whom he had a
warm affection, and in whom he had always placed
the highest confidence. The community, numbering at
least thirty, was made up of men who had followed
him from his monasteries in Burgundy or had joined
him in Bregenz. They set to work to repair the ruins;
the old walls were rebuilt and a new roof put on the
church. Jonas tells us that they received manifest help
from Heaven. ' When the logs happened to fall into
inaccessible crevices in the rocks, where no waggon
could go, Columban, with two or three others, was
able to carry them away on their shoulders, though
thirty or forty could not move those logs on the level
ground.' Soon, enough buildings were ready for their
needs, and the great abbey of Bobbio was started on
its long and glorious career, that lasted down to the
French Revolution. Its library was one of the most
valuable in Europe, but in the course of time was
scattered to other libraries, especially to the Vatican
and the Ambrosian Library of Milan.

Meantime, the prophecies of St. Columban that the
kingdoms of Theodebert and Theoderic would pass to
Clothaire had been fulfilled, and Clothaire found himself in possession of the three kingdoms of Neustria,
Burgundy and Austrasia. He had never forgotten
Columban, and the fulfilment of the prophecy in his
regard made it clearly evident that God was with the
saintly abbot. He had known from personal experience
that no servile awe in the presence of earthly powers
would hinder Columban from denouncing in unmistakable terms any scandals in the courts of kings; but
he had ample evidence, too, of the extraordinary
influence for good that St. Columban had exercised
wherever he went, and determined to do what he could
to procure for his now extensive dominions the benefit

of that great influence. He accordingly sent for Eustasius, now abbot of Luxeuil, whose exalted position and personal affection for St. Columban could be counted on to press the king's request with greater force, and asked him to convey to St. Columban his earnest wish that he return to Luxeuil: he could take with him some of the noblemen of the court, as a guarantee of the king's good intentions, and he would bear all expenses.

The king had made a good selection of a messenger, for none could be more welcome to Columban than Eustasius. On the day of exile at Luxeuil, only the physical force of the soldiers kept Eustasius from following his master. When the opportunity was given him, he hastened to rejoin Columban at Metz, and was with him all the way to Switzerland. From Bregenz Columban sent him back to take over the government of Luxeuil. Speaking of Eustasius, Jonas says: ' Those who had been disciples of St. Columban felt that he was still with them, when they saw the virtues and the customs of the master so faithfully reflected in the disciple.'

Columban was more than pleased to see Eustasius again, and kept him in Bobbio for some weeks, getting all the news from Luxeuil, and availing himself of the opportunity to give further instructions on the duties of an abbot, impressing on him especially the necessity of unity of spirit in the community. Regarding the king's request, he was sorry that he could not fall in with his wishes. His great age would naturally make him slow to undertake any more journeys; but probably the deciding factor was that Bobbio was still in its infancy and would need his guidance more than the solidly established Luxeuil. Though sorry to have to refuse his request, he asked the king to continue to give his royal patronage and assistance to Luxeuil, at the same time repeated the warnings that he had

previously given to the king on his duties to his
Creator. 'Clothaire received his message as a token
of friendship, and did not forget the request that
Columban had made. He protected the monastery of
Luxeuil in every way; he assigned to it a yearly
subsidy; he added to its property as Eustasius
requested, and through love of Columban strove to
further its interests in every way.'

St. Columban was now a very old man, and was
not free from the ills of old age, as he frequently hints
in his poems:

> 'Multa senem fragilis vexant incommoda carnis.
> Nam macie turpi tabescunt languida membra.
> Tunc genuum junctura riget, venasque per
> omnes
> Illius in toto frigescit corpore sanguis.
> Sic baculo nitens artus sustentat inertes.'[40]

It was now more than ever necessary that he should
take to himself the advice he had given to others:

> 'Ultima iam sapiens meditatur tempora vitae'[41];

and as in Annegray and Luxeuil and Bregenz, so here
in Bobbio he had found for himself a place of retire-
ment, in which he could pass some quiet days in meditation and prayer. Tradition points out two caves near
Bobbio to which he was accustomed to retire, where
later oratories were erected, one in honour of Our Lady,
the other in honour of St. Michael. Legend has it that
it was in St. Michael's cave that St. Columban died.
But Jonas does not mention the caves, nor does he give
any detail about St. Columban's death; merely a bare
statement of the fact: 'At length, having spent one
year in the monastery of Bobbio, the blessed Columban
rendered his soul to God, on the ninth day of the
Kalends of December.' As Jonas has given us many a
detailed account of saintly deaths in other monasteries,
we are justified in concluding that the monks in his own

abbey of Bobbio had nothing spectacular to tell him
about the death of St. Columban. The day was
Sunday, November 23rd, 615.

From his writings we can sum up his whole life:

> 'Puerilia desideria fugiens, semper sollicitus,
> semper crescens, semper acquirens; semper
> tendens ad superna, semper currens ad bravium,
> semper coelestia desiderans, semper divina
> sitiens.'

***   ***   ***   ***

> Gradiendum est via regia ad civitatem Dei
> viventis, per afflictionem carnis et spiritus
> humilationem. Vere Christi crucifixi discipuli
> eum sequuntur cum cruce. Fortis in tribulation-
> ibus, audax in causa veritatis.'

When the end was near:

> 'Reddamus Deo nostro, Patri nostro, suam
> imaginem inviolatam in sanctitate, quia ille
> sanctus est';

and he went to join:

> Beata familia
> Quae in altis habitat.
> Laeti letho transacto
> Laetum regem videbunt,
> Cum regnante regnabunt,
> Cum gaudente gaudebunt.
> Tunc dolor, tunc taedium,
> Tunc labor delebitur,
> Tunc Rex regum, Rex mundus
> A mundis videbitur.[42]

CHAPTER XIII.

THE FOUNDATIONS SET FIRM.

IN order to understand how the work of St.
Columban came to have such a prominent place
in the history of the civilization of Western Europe,
it is necessary to say something about its development
under his successors.

Before he left Luxeuil he was, of course, the superior
of all three monasteries. When he left, and even after
the foundation of Bregenz and Bobbio, he was still
abbot of all. We have seen that when Eustasius, the
abbot of Luxeuil, came to him in Bobbio he was
ready to give, and Eustasius was ready to receive,
instructions on the duties of an abbot. After his death
all were independent, though for many years there
continued that strong bond of friendship that arose
from their common origin.

In his letter from Nantes, St. Columban had recommended that Attala be superior of Luxeuil, if he would
consent. Attala, however, refused, and followed St.
Columban through Switzerland and into Italy. It was
natural that after St. Columban's death the monks of
Bobbio would elect as abbot the man whom St.
Columban had chosen.

Attala was a native of Burgundy, of noble family,
and had received from his father a taste for letters.
His early education was entrusted to a bishop named
Aigius; but soon he aspired to higher things, and
entered the monastery of Lerins. He remained in
Lerins for some years, but was not satisfied with the
spirit there, and came to St. Columban in Luxeuil.
We have seen that he elected to share in St.

Columban's wanderings, and succeeded him as abbot of Bobbio.

The early days of Attala's rule in Bobbio were not without trouble. Some of the monks, probably taking advantage of the change of superiors, began to grumble against the strict discipline. Attala did everything to bring them to their senses; he begged them as a father not to leave him, and reminded them that those who had gone before them were now in the enjoyment of Heaven, as a reward for their mortification. But all to no avail, and many left the monastery. But God, in His Providence, would not allow His plans for the great future of Bobbio to be thwarted in those early days, and showed His displeasure so clearly that many repented and begged for readmission. Attala gladly received them back, and peace and unity again reigned in the monastery.

Jonas was minister or secretary to Attala, and so was in a position to know him well, and to hear from him all about the early days in Luxeuil, and the journeys through Switzerland and the foundation of Bobbio. He tells one story about himself. 'I had been about nine years in the monastery, and my people at home had often asked that I be allowed to go and see them; but in vain. Then one day, though no one had suggested anything about it, the abbot said to me: "Go quickly, son, and see your mother and your brother; and, remember, return without delay." When I hesitated and said that to-morrow would be a good day to start—it was February and very cold—he said: "Go at once; you may not be able to go later." My home was at Susa, a fine city, about 120 miles from Bobbio. My mother was delighted to see me after such a long absence. But that night . . . I felt that I was being urged by the prayers not to delay, but to return at once. . . . Next day we set out. . . . When we reached the monastery we found the abbot near death.'

Attala lived only a few days after Jonas' return. ' When the end was near, he asked to be brought outside his cell. He looked up at the crucifix that he had placed there, and began to weep and to sing the praises of the Holy Cross: ''Hail, dear Cross, which has borne the ransom of the world, and has carried the standard of eternity; you have brought to us the remedy for all our wounds; you have been anointed with His Blood, Who, to redeem mankind, descended from Heaven to this vale of tears, and Who, through you, has washed away the stain of the first Adam.'' He then asked that all should retire and leave him alone for a while. All went away except one, whose name was Blimond, who stood quietly behind him, for he was afraid that he might collapse, and he wished to be at hand to help him. When Attala thought that all had gone away, he began to implore God with many tears to have pity on him, though he was unworthy of any mercy; to forgive him his sins and to restore him to grace; and, through His mercy, not to deny him the happiness of Heaven. Then through his tears he saw Heaven open to receive him; for many hours he gazed on this vision, while only heartfelt sighs expressed his deep emotion. He then called the monks to bring him back to his cell. The brother I mentioned told me of the incident that same day.' Next day Attala spoke a few words of exhortation to his monks, and died. In the Roman Martyrology his Feast is on March 10.

The expulsion of St. Columban from Luxeuil had left the administration of that monastery in a very unsettled state. Ultimately, as we have seen, Eustasius was sent back from Bregenz to be superior there.

Eustasius was a Burgundian of noble birth, and in his early days was in the military service of the king. But he tired of the world and entered Luxeuil, where he was appointed head of the school. ' He was held in the highest esteem by all; and those who had been disciples of St. Columban felt that he was still with them, when they saw the virtues and the customs of the master so faithfully reflected in the life of the disciple.' Following the wish of St. Columban, he devoted himself to the preaching of the faith to the pagans. He first worked among the pagans who still remained in the vicinity of Besançon; later he went to the country of the Bavarians, and, when his duties called him home, left other reliable men to carry on the work.

There are a few incidents in the life of St. Eustasius that may not be omitted, as they have direct bearing on the progress of the work of St. Columban.

The reader will remember that in St. Columban's journey eastwards through France he stayed for a while at the home of a man named Chagneric, whose children he blessed, two sons, Chagnoald and Faron, and one daughter, Fara, then an infant. Years later, Chagnoald, then a monk of Luxeuil, was a companion to Eustasius on a journey to the king's court, which was then in the north of France. On their way they visited Chagnoald's home, where they learned to their sorrow that his sister, Fara, was seriously ill, and had lost the sight of her eyes. They also discovered that her father had been trying to force her to marry, though she had been dedicated to God by St. Columban in her infancy. On hearing this Eustasius severely upbraided the father, telling him that his attempt to violate the command of the saint was the cause of his daughter's illness. The father dissimulated and said that his one wish was that his daughter be restored to health, and that she dedicate her life to God. ' Eustasius then went to the girl and asked her whether she wished to set aside the heavenly nuptials counselled by the blessed Columban, and seek again the vows of men. She answered that she had never

F

yielded to such intentions, nor would she exchange the joys of Heaven for those of earth; she had always been ready, and was now ready, to carry out the counsels of the man of God. "Last night," she said, "I saw in a vision a man like you in appearance, who restored my sight; and I heard a voice telling me to do whatever this man would direct, and that I would be cured." Eustasius then fell on his knees and prayed to God to grant their request. He made the Sign of the Cross on her eyes, and the sight was restored. He promised that on his return from the king he would invest her in the religious habit.'

But the father soon forgot his promise and tried again to force her to marry. She heard of his intentions and fled with one of her companions to the basilica of St. Peter. Her father sent his servants after her, with orders to put her to death. To their threats she replied: 'If you think that I am afraid to die, put it to the test here in this church. Gladly would I lay down my life for Him, Who did not refuse to die for me.' Eustasius returned in time to save her. She received the religious habit from the bishop of Meaux, and founded a monastery for nuns on her father's property. Eustasius sent monks from Luxeuil to superintend the building of the monastery; and, when the nuns had taken up residence, he sent her brother Chagnoald and Walbert, who was later abbot of Luxeuil, to instruct them in the rule. This was the first monastery for nuns under the rule of St. Columban. The Feast of St. Fara, sometimes called Burgundofara, is in the Roman Martyrology on April 3.

St. Fara figures also in the following incident, an incident fraught with danger, but destined to be an important turning-point in the history of St. Columban's influence.

A monk in Luxeuil named Agrestius had asked that he be allowed go and preach the faith to the pagans.

He seemed to be a good religious, but Eustasius must have seen some flaw in his character, for he rebuked him severely for thinking that he, who was still practically a novice in the spiritual life, should think himself fit or worthy for such a work: those to be assigned to that work should be eminent in every branch of the religious life; even Jeremias and Moses, when called by God, deemed themselves unworthy. Agrestius continued to urge his request, and Eustasius reluctantly gave permission. He went first to Bavaria, where he remained only a short time, with little success; he was, as Jonas says, ' like a tall plane tree, that shakes its chattering leaves in the wind, but has no fruit.' From there he went to Aquileia, in northern Italy, where he took up the cause of the schismatics.[43] He wrote to St. Attala in Bobbio, but was ignored. (Jonas tells us that he had been given the letter to keep, but that he lost it through carelessness.) He then had the audacity to return to Luxeuil to try to drag Eustasius into the schism, but was driven from the monastery for his pains. His next step, as could have been expected, was to turn his attack against the rule and customs of St. Columban. He succeeded in getting his cousin, Abelenus, the bishop of Geneva, to listen to him, and tried to win over King Clothaire. The king, however, had known St. Columban too well to entertain any charges against him; but, probably with a view to finishing the matter once and for all, he decided to put the whole question before a synod of the bishops of Burgundy. The synod met at Macon, under the presidency of Tretecus, the bishop of Lyons.

At this synod the first charge that Agrestius made was that innovations had been introduced contrary to the canons. When pressed for details, he mentioned making the Sign of the Cross over the spoon used in drinking and the blessing asked on leaving and entering the various sections of the monastery. The bishops saw nothing reprehensible in such customs, and asked Agrestius if he had any other complaints. He replied that Columban had added to the Collects in the Mass. Eustasius was asked for his reply, and said that the Sign of the Cross banished evil spirits, that asking for a blessing on coming in and going out was sanctioned in the Psalms, and that adding Collects in the Mass was customary in all the churches. Agrestius then added that their form of tonsure was peculiar, their script strange and the whole manner of life unique.

At this stage all saw that no serious charge had been made against the rule of St. Columban, and urged Agrestius to make peace. Eustasius agreed to receive him back, if he would stop his foolishness. He pretended to consent, but continued his schemes in an underhand manner. He succeeded in winning to his side, for a short while, two saintly monks from Luxeuil, SS. Romaric and Amatus, the latter of whom was then abbot of the monastery that St. Romaric had founded on his property in Remiremont. (St. Romaric himself was abbot of Remiremont when Jonas wrote.) His efforts to draw St. Fara into his net had no success; her reply left no doubt where she stood: ' Did you come here to poison the good honey of our lives, and to offer us your bitter deadly fare in place of our good wholesome food? You slander those whose virtues I myself have known, whose salutary doctrines I have accepted, and who have led many into the joys of Heaven, as I myself can testify. Give up this foolishness at once.'

Then, as in the early disturbances in Bobbio, Providence showed on which side was the blessing of Heaven. Many of the adherents of Agrestius died suddenly, some by their own hand. Agrestius himself was murdered by a slave that he had ransomed. Amatus and Romaric gave up their opposition and were received back to full friendship by Eustasius.

One great turning-point was now reached, for, in the words of Jonas, 'Abelenus and the other bishops of Gaul were afterwards strong supporters of the institutes of St. Columban, and their esteem for him induced them to found many monasteries where his rule is followed. Among them is the renowned Eloi, the present bishop of Noyon. As he is still alive, I may not speak of him, lest I be accused of flattery.' This silent tribute of Jonas has been endorsed by the Church and by the constant tradition of France, where the name of " *le grand saint Eloi* " has always been a household word. In the Roman Martyrology his Feast is on December 1st.

Eustasius could remember the early days, when some of the neighbouring bishops were a source of great trouble to St. Columban, and were in no small measure responsible for his expulsion from Luxeuil; now he had the happiness of seeing the public vindication of their way of life and its extraordinary expansion throughout France, through the personal enthusiastic energy of the bishops. In a short time more and more sees were filled by those who had received the blessing of St. Columban or had been trained in his monasteries. This is one of the strongest grounds for the claim that 'renaissance of all Christian science and culture in many parts of France, Germany and Italy is due to the labours and zeal of Columban' (Pius XI): that through his example and his teaching he was responsible, under God, for placing so many men of heroic sanctity to rule the monasteries and the dioceses of France in the golden age of the Church in that country.

The great zeal that now inspired the bishops was greatly fostered and intensified, spiritually as well as materially, by the saintly group of men that now formed the court of the king, and not least by the kings themselves. Thus we find the two sources of trouble with which St. Columban had to deal now united in spreading far and wide the rule of life that he had preached.

St. Columban had been in correspondence with the Popes of his time, and had expressed his desire to visit them: ' te, non Romam, desiderans '; but sickness and the duties of his office had prevented him. In spite of a late tradition, it is practically certain that he never visited Rome. Shortly after St. Bertulf had been elected to succeed St. Attala as abbot of Bobbio, he found it necessary to appeal to the Holy See against some claims of the local bishop. He decided to bring the matter personally before Pope Honorius, and Jonas, then his secretary, was one of those who went with him. Here is Jonas' account of what happened:

' When they had stated the cause of their coming, Honorius asked for detailed information about their rule of life. He was pleased at what he heard and at the manifest signs of sound religious spirit and humility. He kept Bertulf with him for some time and encouraged him to continue on the course that he had set and to do all in his power to combat the Arian pest with the sword of the Gospel. Pope Honorius was a man of keen mind, was wise in counsel, of deep learning and richly endowed with the virtues of kindness and humility. He had many a pleasant conversation with Bertulf and was anxious to keep him with him as long as possible. But when the great heat made further stay in Rome inadvisable, the Pope granted Bertulf's request and issued the privilege by which the monastery of Bobbio was withdrawn from the jurisdiction of the bishop.'

On their way home an interesting incident occurred, which consoled Bertulf with the thought that the great Apostle and first Pope, under whose patronage the abbeys of Luxeuil and Bobbio had been established, was watching over him with the same kind sympathy that he had just received from his successor in Rome. Jonas was present and tells us about it. 'We had passed Tuscany and were in the Apennine country when Bertulf was attacked by such a violent fever that his life was despaired of. He had been sick before we left Rome, and the long journey had been too much for him. With very little hope for his recovery, we pitched tent in a wild, rough country. It was the vigil of the feast of SS. Peter and Paul. When night came on, he called me and asked about the preparations for the night. I told him that everything was in order, and he said to me: " You stay here near my couch and watch until morning." But as I watched, and the long night dragged on, so great a drowsiness came over me that I could scarcely keep my head from nodding; and those who were watching the horses and the baggage were equally drowsy. In the silence of the night, the blessed Prince of the Apostles, Peter, came and stood at the couch of the sick man and said to him: " Arise, and return in good health to your friends." Bertulf asked who it was, and heard the answer: " Peter; to-day my feast is being celebrated throughout the world." With these words he departed. Bertulf was stricken with fear and asked me what it was, for he thought that I had seen and heard everything. When I told him that I had not seen anything, he said: " Do you not see the Apostle Peter departing in glory?" I told him that I could not see anything; and he was silent. I then realised that he had seen a vision, and, with some difficulty, I was able to induce him to tell me what had happened; he would never have told his secret, but that he thought that I had seen and heard everything.'

It was thought necessary to add these few pages on the history of the years immediately following the death of St. Columban, in order to show the place that he and his way of life had won in the minds of the kings, the bishops and the Holy See. It is beyond our purpose to follow further the history of his foundations. This much may be said. For some hundreds of years the monasteries founded by St. Columban and his friends were never in need of reform. Sometimes, when the fire in a monastery burned dangerously low, a few torches were brought from Luxeuil, and the fire blazed again. In the time of Charlemagne the administrative structure of the Benedictine rule was made obligatory on all monasteries of France, in much the same way as the Constitutions of various Societies and Congregations have lately been modified by the Holy See. This modification paved the way for the introduction of other phases of Benedictine life, until in time all monasteries were looked upon as part of the Benedictine family.

ST. COLUMBAN'S LETTER.

TO HIS MOST DEAR SONS AND FOLLOWERS, TO HIS BROTHERS IN TRIAL, TO ALL HIS MONKS, COLUMBAN, A SINNER, SENDS GREETINGS IN CHRIST.

PEACE be to you, as the good Lord wished His disciples, and salvation and unending charity. That the Blessed Trinity may grant you these blessings and preserve them among you is my most earnest prayer. He alone who inspired me, only He knows how I long for your salvation and for your continued progress in the knowledge of God. But now, seeing that Our Lord's words have come to pass in our regard, that suffering and persecution would come because of the Gospel, I feel that I should warn you to be careful lest the good seed may find in your hearts a rocky soil, that can produce nothing but a weak and sickly plant, and the Lord say of you: "When tribulation and persecution arose because of the word, forthwith they were scandalized."[17] We know with what joy and gladness we received the word of God: let us be careful not to show ourselves believers only for a time. We have need of patience, that the proving of our faith may be more precious than gold.[18] Remember that our fight is not for trivial things, but for the kingdom of Heaven; and to fight for a kingdom is nothing new among men. Do not delude yourselves by thinking that it is only against men that you fight; the devils resent all that God has done for you and are in this fight also. Against them put on the armour of God, as St. Paul urges,[19] and fight your way to Heaven, overcoming your enemies with the arrows of fervent prayer. Whatever you all ask together with faith will be given to you. But be careful to be of one mind and one heart, that you may receive, even now, whatever graces you ask of the Father of Our Lord Jesus Christ, the common Father of us all, as Our Lord has said: " If two of you shall consent upon earth, concerning any thing whatsoever they shall ask, it shall be done to them by my Father who is in Heaven."[20]

If you be not of one mind and one heart, it were better that you be not together. Therefore I enjoin on you all, all who would be of one mind with me, to take Attala as your superior. He may decide for himself whether to remain in Luxeuil or to follow me. If he decides to follow me, let Waldalenus be your prior. In the meantime, be careful that you have none among you, no matter who he is, who is not of one mind and one heart with you; we have had enough trouble with men of that kind.

You know, my dear Attala, those who may cause trouble. Send them away at once, but with all charity and as the rule prescribes. Hold Libranus in high esteem, and always keep Waldalenus with you; may God bless him and keep him truly humble; say good-bye to him for me: I had no chance of seeing him in all the excitement. You know how eager I was to bring others closer to God. If you find that you can do good by staying in Luxeuil, stay there; but if you see serious trouble ahead, come away; I mean trouble arising from discord. I am afraid that trouble may arise about the Easter question. They may think that without me you would be more open to attack, and try to cause trouble, at the instigation of the devil.

Be careful, therefore, and instruct one another and those who are willing to learn. But have no one among you who is not of one mind with you. Above all things have peace, being 'careful to keep the unity of the Spirit in the bond of peace.'[21] Quid enim prodest habere corpus, et non habere cor? Unity of body is nothing without unity of heart.

I must confess, Attala, that I was almost broken in spirit by my efforts to help all: 'when I spoke to them they fought against me without cause'[22]; in my trust of everyone I almost became a fool. You should be more prudent; I would not have you suffer under that burden as I did. You will realise now that you must accommodate your teaching to each individual, because men differ so much one from another. But what is this that I am doing? I am urging you to take on a burden that I am running away from. I will merely call attention to the necessity for diversity in instruction. Therefore try to accommodate yourself to the needs of all, all who obey you in truth and love. And their very love for you may be a danger. You see, there are dangers on both sides. If they hate you, peace is at an end; their love for you may be a danger to good administration. Keep clearly before your mind the one end for which we should work, the end on which you know that I had set my heart: the salvation of many souls, unto the building up of the Lord, that is, His Church. My own natural inclination was to serve God in a life of solitude. I pray that, now that I am absent, you will be able to do what I only wished, bring many more souls into the Church of God.

I am writing this letter, because I do not know what the future may bring. It was my intention that we should go and preach the Gospel to the pagans, though what I heard of their indifference nearly discouraged me. When I began to write this letter my mind was running in a rather mournful mode; but I remembered that you had enough troubles to cope with, and decided to write in a different strain; to check your tears rather than provoke them. I have tried to conceal my grief. The tears are near, but we must check them; tears are not the mark of a good soldier. What has happened to us is nothing new; the Gospels are full of examples; in fact, one of the great truths that the Gospels teach us is, that the true disciple of Christ crucified must take up his cross and follow Him. A wonderful example has been given to us, and a sacred mystery has been made known to us: the Son of God freely ascended the Cross, as a criminal—' He was offered because it was his own will '[23]—as it is written, leaving us an example that we should follow His steps.'[24] Blessed therefore is he who shares in His sufferings and His humiliations. In this there is a wonderful mystery, for ' the foolishness of God is wiser than men, and the weakness of God is stronger than men.'[25] The highest wisdom is seen in foolishness, and in weakness courage beyond compare. These truths, these mysteries of our salvation, are the source of all our consolations. They are hard to accept, and so are of greater merit; they are strange and obscure, and therefore appeal only to the few. Let us then suffer with patience, that we may share in the sufferings of Our Lord: ' If we suffer, we shall also reign with Him.'[26]

What more do we need but to persevere? ' He that shall persevere to the end, he shall be saved.'[27] At the end is the judgment, and it is only then that anyone can be praised. In order to persevere, let each one pray to God for help in all humility: ' It is not of him that willeth, nor of him that runneth, but of God that showeth mercy.'[28] Greater and better is the mercy of God than the life of man,[29] however good it may be. None are worthy of mercy but those who confess their helplessness before God, by whose mercy they have been saved from utter ruin. For, though they may know that they have done some good, yet they cannot forget their sins, and, fearing the judgment, place all their hope in the fatherly love of God. The more our fear of God is founded in true humility, the more pleasing it is to God: ' The Lord taketh pleasure in them that fear Him, and in them that hope in His mercy.'[30]

No one can be saved by his own right hand, as the Lord said to Job, when He gave him examples of His own almighty power, and showed him how ridiculous were his attempts to justify himself: ' Then I will confess that thy right hand is able to save thee.'[31] He only will be justified who, in all humility, will make use of the gifts that God has given him, in fear and trembling and according to the will of God; he whose constant prayer is: ' Cast me not away from Thy face '[32]; and ' Let me not stray from Thy commandments.'[33] It has been said that great virtue has been the occasion of ruin to some, meaning that when their sanctity began to be talked about they lost their humility. Therefore it is written: ' Whom dost thou excel in beauty? Go down and sleep with the uncircumcised ';[34] as if He said: Because you have proudly exalted yourself in your sanctity, go down now and be reckoned among sinners, for I will not regard what is done through pride. The gate, you see, is narrow and the way of perfection is followed by few; on the left is vice, and on the right pride and vanity. We must walk the royal road to the city of the living God by mortification of the flesh and contrition of heart; by labour of the body and humility of soul; by zeal in carrying out our duties, not by any merit of our own; and, what is greater than these, by the grace of Christ, in faith and hope and charity. There are many dangers to fear from the flesh. But keep in mind what you are fighting for, and the great glory that is to come. The enemy is strong, and your will is free, giving him an opening to attack. Without an enemy there can be no fight; and without a fight, no crown. Therefore we must be strong and watchful, zealous and patient, faithful and wise, steadfast and prudent; if not, defeat and ruin.

You see, my dear Attala, how we are tossed about by dangers on all sides. In the rush of the whirlpool we are buffeted about, and even in our own hearts we are constantly under attack from the enemy. In such great dangers it is, in one sense, in our power to ' will and to run '; but in another sense, it is not. Left to itself, weak human nature cannot conquer such formidable enemies, but must depend on the mercy of God to win its fight and to finish its course in triumph, conquering its own weakness and the thousand enemies that assail it. In order to merit we must have humility, for without humility we will not receive the help we need. The proud man does not merit, but is left helpless in the hardness of his heart. The ungrateful who do not pray are useless servants; the lazy man is punished even in this life; the little he does is despised, and he scarcely deserves to be called a man.

What can we say, then. We, who before we have given up our sinful habits, are already boasting of our vitrues; we think we are well on the road to perfection, even before we have given up sin. We are very keen to learn what we should do, but very slow to put into practice what we learn. Such an attitude may have some value in things of this world, but it has no value before God. There it is not he who speaks, but he who acts, who will be saved.

And now, as I write, they have come to tell me that the ship is ready, to bring me back to my native land against my will. They seem to have taken no precautions to prevent my escape; it looks as if they wished that I should escape. If like another Jonas—that is the word in Hebrew for Columba—if I am cast into the sea, may there be some one like the whale, to bring your Jonas safe ashore. Though I had much more to say, I find that I have come to the end of my parchment. There is very little order in this letter, but love knows nothing about order. I had intended to put all I had to say in a few words, but I could not. May God's will be done in all things.

Examine into your own lives honestly and clearly, whether you are more detached from things of this world and nearer to God in my absence. Do not come after me through any affection you may have for me, but only if you think that I can be any help to you. I hope that the troubles that have come upon us will not give rise to divisions among you. Do not be tempted to look for greater freedom, because such freedom will only make you the slaves of sin. He is mine who loves unity; he is not mine who separates; as Our Lord has said: 'He who gathereth not . . . ., scattereth.'[35] If you find that your progress is not what it used to be, and if I am still separated from you, and Attala does not wish to be your superior, let all come together in some suitable place and elect some one to be superior for the time being; if it is the will of God that I be set free, I will take care of you. If the location is suitable, and if God builds with you, may you increase, with the blessing of Heaven, to thousands of thousands.[36] And pray for me, my good friends, that I may live to God.

ST. COLUMBAN'S INSTRUCTION
ON CHARITY

Moses wrote in the Law: 'God made man to His own image and likeness.' I would ask you to consider the great dignity that is here implied. The omnipotent God, who cannot be seen by mortal eyes nor comprehended by the mind of man, whose infinite perfections are beyond the power of tongue to utter, when He made man from the dust of the earth, ennobled him with the dignity of His own image. What is man to God? or the dust of the earth to a spirit? It is, indeed, a great honour that God should deign to bestow on man the image of His eternal life.

As long as man retains this image of God in his soul, he remains elevated to an extraordinary degree of dignity; but if he lose it, utter ruin follows. When a man makes wrong use of the gifts that God has given him, he mars and, as far as in him lies, destroys that image of God; when we use His gifts properly, we are like to Him. He has commanded us to dedicate to Him all the powers that He has given us. This is the first commandment, that we should love God with all our heart, because He first loved us, even before we were born, and from all eternity. By our love of God we renew His image in our souls; and we love Him by keeping His commandments: 'If you love Me, keep My commandments.' He has also commanded us to love one another: 'This is My commandment, that you love one another, as I have loved you.' But true love must be, not merely in word, but in deed and in truth. Let us, therefore, preserve for God, our

Father, His own image pure in holiness, for He is holy; in charity, for He is charity; in love and truth, for He is loving and faithful.

Let us be careful that no image but that of God take shape in our souls. The man who is cruel or headstrong or proud is forming in himself the image of a tyrant. Just as there can be false doctrine in the written word, so also can there be a false or spurious image in the soul. Truth differs from error, and justice from wickedness; charity from hatred, and zeal from sloth; virtue from vice, and true love from hypocrisy. Virtue and vice cannot exist together; neither can peace and discord. If we would have peace, let us not allow the image of a tyrant to form in our souls, but rather let Christ form His own image in us, for He has said: 'Peace I leave with you, My peace I give unto you.'

It is of little advantage for us to know that peace is a blessing, if we do not carefully guard it. Usually whatever is of great value is very fragile, and needs to be very carefully protected. And what is impaired by even the slightest word against our neighbour is very fragile indeed. We injure no one when we speak kindly of them; and we do not speak kindly of those whom we despise. If you say: 'Thou fool,' you have violated peace and are 'in danger of hell fire.' Therefore, we must be ever on our guard to observe the law of brotherly love, and restrain our tongues from thoughtlessly giving utterance to whatever happens to come into our minds; we will have to render an account, not only for injurious words, but even for idle words. Try to curb all inclination to incessant talk; it would be better to confine yourself to what is necessary. There is nothing that men like better than discussing what does not concern them, and talking about the faults of their neighbour. It is better

G

to be silent, if one cannot truthfully apply to oneself
the words: ' The Lord hath given me a learned tongue,
that I should know how to uphold by word him that is
weary.' (Isa. 50, 4). Be careful that in all your words
you safeguard peace.

Even the most prudent will offend less if they speak
less. He who is guilty of lying or cursing or detraction
turns his own sword against himself. And what does
our enemy like better than that we fall at our own
hands! See what happens when we sin! The structure
that we have laboured long and hard to build, with the
help of the grace of God, can be levelled to the ground
by one word of detraction. We never speak badly of
those we love; detraction is born of hate, and the
offspring of such a father must be exterminated.

My dear friends, that community is in danger where
those sins are not avoided. The Apostle says: ' If you
bite and devour one another: take heed you be not
consumed one of another.' (Gal. 5, 15). And if he
who does not love is in death (I John, 3, 14), where
will he be who is guilty of the sin of detraction? This
is a matter for tears rather than words. On what does
the law of God insist more strongly and more
frequently than on love? And how seldom do we meet
with it! What excuse have we to offer? Surely we
cannot say that it is too hard or too exacting. Love is
not hard. Rather, it brings peace and comfort and
strength to our souls. If the soul be not dead in sin,
love invigorates it, and makes it dear to God; for
nothing is dearer to God than this love of charity;
as the Apostle says, it is the fulfilment of the law and
the commandments of God: ' He that loveth his
neighbour hath fulfilled the law.' (Rom. 13, 8). He
who fulfils the law by his zealous observance of
charity, has eternal life, as St. John says: ' We know
that we have passed from death to life, because we

love the brethren. He that loveth not abideth in death. Whosoever hateth his brother is a murderer. And you know that no murderer hath eternal life abiding in himself.' (I John, 3, 14, 15). If, then, we do not love, we cannot hope to escape punishment. The fulfilment of the law is charity: may He who deigns to give it, inspire our hearts with it abundantly, Our Lord and Saviour, Jesus Christ, the Lord of peace and the God of charity, to whom be glory for ever. Amen.

TRANSLATION FROM THE MONOSTICHA.

Most worthy is the soul that is clothed in the love of Christ.

Let no one live for oneself, but always for Christ.

You who love Christ should be zealous for His interests, not your own.

Let the tongue have its reins firmly bound in the heart.

Control of the tongue is a great virtue.

Be not hasty in speech, nor slothful in act.

Against a chatterer do not contend in words.

When you judge another, first examine your own life.

Pass judgment on your own faults, rather than on another's.

Beware lest in success you have cause to repent.

No one can be praised unreservedly before the day of death.

Never desert a friend in time of adversity.

He who hopes to see his wishes fulfilled, should first fulfil the wishes of God.

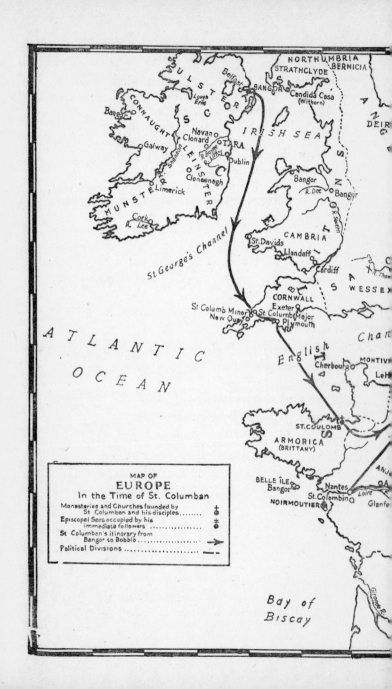

MAP OF
EUROPE
In the Time of St. Columban

Monasteries and Churches founded by
St Columban and his disciples........
Episcopal Sees occupied by his
immediate followers ....
St Columban's itinerary from
Bangor to Bobbio ....
Political Divisions ....

FOOTNOTES.

[1] For questions dealing with life in the Irish monasteries, see Father Ryan's *Irish Monasticism*.

[2] The Rule of Bangor is good:
   It is sound and blessed by God;
   Strict, holy and unchanging,
   Exalted, just and admirable.

[3] Genesis, 12, 1.

[4] The main motive that prompted Irishmen of the time to leave their native land was their desire to offer an additional sacrifice to God. Doubtless, other motives were also present. St. Columban tells us that his wishes were to preach to the pagans and to lead a solitary life.

[5] This monastery, about which very little is known, was at Saulcy, about ten miles south of Annegray.

[6] The location of this place is not known.

[7] From this we can learn how St. Columban's third foundation had grown in a very few years.

[8] Cf. the opening words of the chapter on discretion in St. Columban's Rule : '' The mistakes of many and the ruin of some show us how necessary discretion is for monks. Those who began without this virtue, and whose lives were not regulated by its controlling wisdom, were not able to continue to a praiseworthy end. Those who live without discretion are always in danger of falling into excess, on one side or the other; and true virtue is the mean.''

[9] The full text of this letter is given below, pp.   .

[10] Most worthy is the soul that is clothed in the love of Christ.'

[11] ' Complete and not partial.'

[12] Cf. his sympathy for St. Attala on appointing him superior of Luxeuil. Below p.

[13] From the Instruction on the Love of God and of our neighbour. Migne 80, 251.

[14] The last words of the Rule.

[15] Gal. 5, 15.

[16] Eccli. 34, 23.

[17] Matt. 13, 21.

[18] 1 Peter, 1, 7.

[19] Eph. 6, 13, 17.

[20] Matt. 18, 19.

[21] Eph. 4, 3.

[22] Ps. 119, 7.

[23] Isaias 53, 7.

[24] 1 Peter, 2, 21.

[25] 1 Cor., 1, 25.

[26] 2 Tim., 2, 12.

[27] Matt. 10, 22.

[28] Rom. 9, 16.

[29] Ps. 62, 4.

[30] Ps. 146, 11.

[31] Job 40, 9.

[32] Ps. 50, 13.

[33] Ps. 118, 10.

[34] Ezech. 32, 19.

[35] Luke 11, 23.

[36] Gen. 24, 60.

[37] There is a church in Dublin dedicated in honour of St. Audoen. His feast is in the Roman Martyrology on August 24.

[38] ' Our ship, fashioned from the forest, is borne along on the waters of the branching Rhine, and is washed by its waves. Ho! men: and echo answers Ho!

The King of hosts, the fountain of creation, the all-mighty, is with him who fights, and gives the prize to the victor. Remember Christ, and let your voices cry Ho!'

[39] ' Weighed down by bitter infirmities, which I suffer in my frail body, in sad old age I have come to my eighteenth Olympiad.' The word ' Olympiad ' may mean either a period of four years or of five. We cannot be certain which St. Columban meant.

[40] ' Many a malady of the weak body disturbs the old. The sickly members grow weak and waste away. The knees are stiff, and through all the veins the blood runs sluggishly.' *Thus leaning on a staff*

[41] ' The wise man meditates on the end of life.' *he supports his inactive limbs.*

[42] Putting aside the pleasures of youth, ever watchful, ever growing, ever gleaning. Always stretching to what is above, and running for the prize; always longing for the joys of Heaven, and thirsting for the gifts of God. The royal road to the city of the living God is through subjection of the flesh and humility of spirit. In truth, the disciples of the crucified Christ follow Him with the Cross. Strong in time of trouble, daring in the cause of truth.

Let us return to God, our Father, His own image in all holiness, for He is holy.

. . . The blessed company, who live in Heaven. When death has passed, gladly will they see the King of all gladness; with Him will they reign, with Him will they rejoice. Then sorrow and languor and toil will be ended; then the King of Kings, the King of all purity, will be seen by the pure of heart.

[43] See above pp. 73 seqq.